FOREVER SPOKEN

The International Library of Poetry

Howard Ely, Editor

Forever Spoken

Proudly manufactured in the United States of America by
The International Library of Poetry
One Poetry Plaza
Owings Mills, MD 21117

poetry.COM
The International Library of Poetry

FOREWORD

Throughout life, we store information collected from experiences and try in some way to make sense of it. When we are not able to fully understand the things that occur in our lives, we often externalize the information. By doing this, we are afforded a different perspective, thus allowing us to think more clearly about difficult or perplexing events and emotions. Art is one of the ways in which people choose to externalize their thoughts.

Within the arts, modes of expression differ, but poetry is a very powerful tool by which people can share sometimes confusing, sometimes perfectly clear concepts and feelings with others. Intentions can run the gamut as well: The artists may simply want to share something that has touched their lives in some way, or they may want to get help to allay anxiety or uncertainty. The poetry within *Forever Spoken* is from every point on the spectrum: every topic, every intention, every event or emotion imaginable. Some poems will speak to certain readers more than others, but it is always important to keep in mind that each verse is the voice of a poet, of a mind that needs to make sense of this world, of a heart that feels the effects of every moment in this life, and perhaps of a memory that is striving to surface. Nonetheless, recalling our yesterdays gives birth to our many forms of expression.

Lying by Daisies

Sunday before Valentine's was the last day I'd seen him.
Last glimpse, last hug, last "I love you."
His heart killed him.
Now, sorrowed water trickles down my cheeks.

My clothes are black, and my heart is skipping.
They carry the casket, one thousand men cry.
I'm dazed, pretending to be okay,
and walk out the door following him.
They gave me daisies at the door, his favorite flower.

They stay alive for three weeks, but I want to die.
I'm pretending to be okay, but I'm not.
My heart has drained my body's emotion.
My eyes are stained red,
with black rings underneath them.

The pain struggles to leave my family.
My mom drives past daises and my eyes fill with tears.
"Are you okay?"
"Yes."
But I know I am lying by the daisies.

Danielle Renee Palmer

Untitled

The thick, tangled hillside
slopes down to the creek bed.
I've been on this hillside before.
I've raised my apron to the wind
to set sail in the early evening sky,
searching the dusky shadows below
for my lover.

Wearing a long red skirt,
I've pushed my dark curly hair
from my face and waited.

I've seen my own grandmother
on this hillside.
She was young
with her hair softly pinned up.
She, too, raised her apron to the wind,
setting sail
to await the arrival of her lover.

We smiled at one another.

Jo Anne Barrish

Pleasantly Unpleasant Life

As if the dew has drifted away in the dark night,
the clouds float to their journey's never-ending finish,
rolling on in an eternal butterfly's flight;
even rose bushes pass for a season with only one wish.

As spring brings light to winter's dark dream,
ocean waves continuing with fervent persistence,
birds flying away forever, or so a season would seem,
nostalgic longing for a previous existence.

As tiny circles combine like bubbles floating in space,
galaxies collide and burst into fragments;
the clash of the mountain snow penetrating the land beneath,
fires destroy but beautify beyond the ash.

To find a diamond, one looks for coal;
trusting in the unpredictable has beautiful consequences.

Justen Gregory Watkins

Children of the Wind

Caressing her legs,
playing with her hair
just as he did
two summers ago,
after he escaped
and came to shelter her
when her roof blew away
from a shack without windows
by a river without water.

An eternity of sighs
that echoed her dreams
before they took him back
to barbed wire and butterflies,
while she stood still,
gathering water for the river,
while the wind moaned for her
and whispered in his ear
faraway things he couldn't see.

Asoka Nimal Jinadasa

My Best Friend

All the things we did together,
We could do again.
Your big green eyes,
Your shoulder length hair,
The way you laugh and smile.

We shared the good times,
And the bad.
I will always remember my best friend.
I thought we would never part.

But now you have grown
And moved away.
You have found someone to care for you,
And share the things you like to do.

But don't forget I will always be there for you:
To listen to what you have to say,
To share your joys and your tears,
Your sorrow your pain.

So when you're alone, think of me,
Or even give me a call,
I am not far: I am your loving mum.

Diane Bowler

Air Ballet

You stand poised and stately,
Atop the pole beside the marina.
Neck stretched and almost on tip toe,
You launch yourself gracefully,
Wings stretched wide.
Behind you the pole dances wildly
Belying the gentle energy seemingly exerted,
Gliding gently and smoothly down to sea level.
The smooth sea absorbs you
As you dip to find lunch,
A good meal found,
Return to the pole once more.
Sun drying feathers speedily in gentle breeze;
For one so large, you defy gravity.
In these gentle climes,
A pelican's life seems easy.

Madeline Cameron

In the Wetlands

A kestrel stills, then beats its wings again,
Above the melaleucas, white and black;
It's cool and damp on this green shady track,
Though hot and dry out on the treeless plain.
The creek flows smooth and calm with last month's rain;
The trees look down; their mirrored selves look back.
As ducks come arrowing by my half-seen shack,
Reflections, sundered, seek their shapes in vain.
Magpies carol, crows discordant jeer;
Along the banks, crabs click, bees hum, frogs creak.
Like speaks to like, and makes his meaning clear
Because it's in their common tongue they speak.
Oh, were it so between us two today!
Words can conceal much more than they convey.

Jean Mary Paterson

Etude on Memory

It was heard as a distant chime
Whispering faintly in fatigue
Even as evening clouds climb
Over molding hills in critique
I wasn't there on foreign land
Mesmerized with intrigue
Should memory willingly expand
Embracing a questioned technique
How could such event even arise
From undisturbed times askew
My soul must, in senility, demise
Returning to a world I once knew
Oh clear the tune; now is sublime!
Strain not memory's effort in prime
Litienmin

Richard J. Lee

Silence

Those moments before you spoke were bliss.
You've disturbed them;
You've chapped the lips
Of silence.
The atmosphere has become tense,
The euphonic atmosphere
Of silence.

Helen Williams

Pollination

So, could I have kissed you
that night, that year
when your honey lips hived
around those buzzing words and
tight-knit worker jeans clung to their queen?
Yellow-black bars didn't warn these glaze eyes
of the swoop, the sting,
and fuzzy, busy hands-on swell,
as your abdomen and feeling stuck in me
as you broke
from yourself, again
in a good way, that broken piece you knew you'd regenerate,
your stimulated mouth
hymning that black road. Could you tell
it was seven below?
That Blond Boy wasn't there?
That any word lay outside my fingers
in your hair?

Andrew Shaun Millichip

Timetable

In due time, a span of time, in the
course of a lifetime, inside a millennium.
When, meantime, while just standing there dilly-
dallying, passing time, wasting time, and
killing time, but only for the time being.
Yet at the whole time, creeping,
crawling, and sliding, never at any time
stopping to ask for time. However, at some
time or other, in complete disregard of time
altogether.
I stop at hang time simply because it
requires too much time to talk about time
at any given time.

Gil Prado

Cold Earth

The bricks of the asylum slowly crumble
Away from mist and
Clouds pummeling into cold earth.
Maybe she'll shed her skin like her
Slithering children dancing with midnight.
Soft and out the shell cracks
And the mountains roar with their firm fury.
Once, there stood upon the spike
Of a hill such strength of ignorance
And a blockade of chemicals seeping
Through walls, a soulless building stood
To contain so dangerous a ghost,
Drugged with ennui since first sight,
That no chance may stir a slumbering dragon
So close to a dark death,
Breathing barely a particle
After each cycle the moon completes.
Her skin so cold,
Warmed only by firm fingers
Crawling down and up the flesh.

Michael Wery

Ringo Point

This gravel road leads to Ringo Point.
How many years have you been left here
to wander between walls of aging wire?
And every so often, a woman passes
through an old cattle gate to adorn your
dwelling place with sweet gardenia.
She tells you how your children have grown,
and how they have children now, and
she is sorry that you can't be with them.
She thanks you for letting her keep
your father for a little while longer.
He wanted to be with you, you know.
She lingers by our bedside, then
kneels nearby to see Baby Gregory,
who slipped away long before you.
She asks you, as she always does,
to please watch over him, and us.
And it's easier to leave this time,
as you carry her on downy wings
away from Ringo Point.

Jennifer Hartje

Arizona High Country

She lives in a land of melted quartz,
toothpick pines and the dust of snow,
white as old time.

She drives on roads painted pink with
dripping stone and bridges branching rock.

She sees footprints of ancestors in
waterfalls growing like a trellis
and ice frozen in caves like
sleeping bears.

It is a land of place over people and
peace over pain. A land where truth
is bright as an animal's glare and
deep as a mountain's dirt.

She feels her skin like bark and
smells her hair like sun and knows
she is home.

Jeannette Lynne Kindernay

They Came

I touched words
fingered their curves and corners
their smooth rigidness
tasting their artificial substance
regurgitating their bitterness

I yearned for words taken
called them back screaming and shouting
looked for new ones
searching wide-eyed

I grasped words
held tight their funny motions
shoved them down my parched throat
quenching thirst

I pinned words
the slithering motion of my fingers
expelled the blotchy ink

I think in verse, a hymn of praise
trap words
on the white lined cage
with lessons of life
and unknown expression

Marion Jennifer Hernon

Station, Winter

The sound of trains steaming the air.
The smudge of a kiss abandoned on his cheek
where he has forgotten to remember to shave.
The blue-black glass of ice bruising the skin of windows
where lines of empty-beaked birds stick their eyes to the sills,
dull question marks wondering about crumbs
and the dubious abrupt stillness of iron rails.
The snow of slippery footprints forming the fragments of angel
wings, a staggering celestial walkway of forgettable beauty.
Red sunflowers, the color of collapsing stars, unavoidable to
the eye, snagging sight on their blood petals as she tucked them
beneath her coat.
Her shoe tipping the hem of her skirt as she rose up a step,
a brief slender flutter of silk.
The sudden shrill of whistles, breathless sputter of train
engines and furnaces and the faint tinkling of coal,
blurry fingers tossed into the sky as she waved,
a smile half-hidden by frost and the cloud's gray glare.
The hard fact of her face, same as every other time he had seen
her, even though it was the last.
The things he felt less painful than everything he did not.

Maryse Meijer

Under the Trees in Fort Defiance

Stars winked; a bright moon smiled
through towering oaks pulling forth a tide
of thoughts hidden
in treasured craters of our minds.
Sat upon a high perched swing
sipping on a soft summer night;
we swung through an eon
of time that only we could taste.
At one with Gaia, our laughter
rang through the canopy;
early adventures recalled,
future possibilities embraced
for tomorrows. And tomorrow's
rapturously free and yet to be.

J. Brown

Harvest of the Nets

In a dream, I was standing by the sea,
And Jesus came and He stood by me.
He said to cast a net into the water,
For the catch will be plentiful, my daughter.
I saw fish of every color and size,
They were jumping from the sea against the sunrise.
Jesus said, "See the vision of your dream,
For the harvest of many will soon be seen,
I want my people to cast their nets,
For the blood I shed had paid their debts.
Many souls are waiting to be saved,
To see the land for which I've made.
Cast your nets upon the sea of souls,
For my blood is enough to pay their tolls.
Make haste to the harvest of the nets,
Your hard work will leave no regrets.
Cast my love upon the open water,
And see it return to you, my daughter.
The nets are ready and the sea is full,
A soul that is saved is a precious jewel."

Karen Denise Dorman

Come Back to Me

Come back to me.
Can you hear me beyond that wall,
That curtain of fog,
That haze, that maze, that daze
You hide behind?

Come back to me
And we will drink new wine
Under the eucalyptus tree;
Feeding each other cheese
And licking our fingers like children.

Come back to me.
Whisper words of love
As we share a pillow
And the moon covers us in silver silence.
Tell me again that I am your true love
And look into my eyes
So that I know I am not dreaming.
Come back to me.

Raynette Eitel

To Perceive the Observer

On the corner, he stands,
khaki pants, T-shirt black,
a silver necklace,
holding a silver six-point star with a hole in its center,
Nosoroma,
symbolic for a child of God.
He stands as a solider, erect, on guard:
to protect the contents of urban blight,
keeping the inhabitants in place
as a corrections officer, watching over inmates,
the prisoner of poverty, preventing escape or such hope?
He stands with counterfeit calm, ready to attack,
awaiting the proper, improper order,
standing ready to attack
the natives or invaders?
He is a student,
studying the creatures of the ghetto-wasteland,
creatures that are his cousins, ancestors?
With no discernible destination, taking no action to advance,
(he is I, I am so . . .)
he stands.

Ra Saheb

Photograph

My reasons for being here
are so that you can look at me and shatter
the glass you hold in your hand,
and let your anger consume you
because it's what you love best
(next to your bottle of vodka
and your useless excuses).
I will not go; I love to taunt you
at the end of the night when you fall over,
intoxicated by the lack of someone concrete
and too much clearness.
Crawling up to your room
on broken knees and stained hands,
you don't dare look back,
because you know I am watching and waiting
for another reason to laugh.

Laura Constantinescu

The Shoes

These are the shoes that she shuffled about in,
That had laces which
She learnt to tie.
These are the ones which went through the puddles
In the autumn and the spring.

These are the shoes which we went out in
When her head was filled with questions,
When she declared,
"Shoes, not sooes" and
"Socks, not sots."

These are not the shoes
That she walked across the street in
All alone.
But we'll need them later
For her new sister,
Whom she'll never know.

Ahmed Shams Chowdhury

God's Land

I am a walrus of a vision
In shades of mediocrity
The chasms I drew
Lay in bounds
Forfeited by time itself
Irrefutable the intoxicating smile
Of dawn burst forth
Continents awoke
Melting pots overran
Where glaciers once kissed
A liquid spear split the plates apart
Golden soil for crimson races
Silent gases from magma faces
Pods of dreams which will soon
Flourish into valleys of green
The name of this place
America

David Smith

A Milliner's Widow

As he died, she dreamed,
Rose above the Absalom.

Let slip the tailor's hand,
Shroud his lupine stare.
Then weeping, drew back her feral hair.

Strayed blind afore the altar,
To light a trembling cigarette.

I held there the angel's silhouette.
Caught brief, her pale dominion
Through a valley of penitent man.

Others drew the light in,
And shook the rags of Prague.

As Kaddish halls diminish
And morphine taps absolve me,
I rest my weary vigil
Within the breath of God.

S. John Wood

The Battle

Violent clamourings locked within,
A thousand squirming worms,
Burrowing through loops and coils,
Sealing the light, the warmth, the sun

Paired voices, incessantly
Orchestrating my downfall,
Gnawing away with the
Assurance of validity

The proud stammering defense,
Weakens, stretches an arm
Like a drowning man
That is finally pulled under

The glimmer of hope,
Smothered, snuffed out,
Crumpled, exhausted,
Defeated again.

Louise Yvonne Clare

Library Books Like Tombstones

Library books like tombstones
lined in a row still await
the visit of a family member,
a friend, or even a stranger
to pay homage to a restless soul.

Titles on library volumes,
like names engraved on a stone,
recite the record of voices
calling from the depth of the Earth
to be saved from the wrath of oblivion.

Though many will visit the graveyard,
and many will read out the names,
only a few will discover
the messages waiting entombed
in the cemetery of stones without graves.

Emil Jacob

Traitor

Realizing the truth is hard.
For some, impossible,
Yet, it's still true.
While we were young,
Friendship is all that mattered.
Later, my lipstick outlined your lips,
Smeared on your shirt.
Laughter.
But now silence is all to be heard.
An occasional sigh.
No tears, no "sweet child, don't cry, mama's here."
Sickly sweet lies; roses with thorns.
Your scent mixed with an unfamiliar perfume
from a tiny glass bottle I do not own.
The shirt with the traces
of my lipstick is now foreign,
her lipstick outlines the lips of the traitor.

Gina Nicole Boyd

Scissors

You gave me scissors
to cut the bond between us,
a tool to do the deed
you did not wish to be
attributed to you.

Saundra Akers

Beneath Tasha's Tree

Gazing through the branches and leaves
Rustling, whistling a gentle breeze.
Seeking shelter for a little while,
Hoping to regain her inner child.

Escaping from all the demands,
Responsible only for the task at hand.
Time to think and contemplate
A new existence, a different fate.

Seeing all yet not being seen,
Hidden in nature's camouflaged scene.
Time to reflect on all that is true,
Thoughts as clear as the sky is blue.

Climbing down to confront her fear,
A new reality could suddenly appear.
Touching the soil, her heart set free,
Safe and sound beneath Tasha's tree.

Michele Dionne

Facing Peabody Conservatory

Oscillating sprinklers spraying the bright green summer leaves,
The bronze statue and the ring of pink petunias,
Droplets trickling down from the tree's limbs,
The spouts splashing into the fountain, like someone peeing
In the toilet, the ripples resembling shiny gold doubloons
Slate-colored pigeons nestling in the grass,
Their tiny eyes orange
Like the Dr. Seuss-like fish sculpture that faces
St. Paul Street,
The growling of a black and tan chunky-headed Rottweiler,
Who probably weighed as much as I do
A thin, bespectacled dark-skinned man with a stud in his ear
Walked by, glanced at me, then began singing "Wade in the Water"
Another man in blue plaid shirt and jeans drank the fountain
Water spouting from the mouth of a stone lion-faced gargoyle
He dipped inside the water fully clothed then came back out,
Soaked, of course
My first impression was that he intended to drown himself

Medina Krause

Time's Maze

The square . . .
Plaza life, striped with polka-dotted, purple pilgrimages,
So bright with neon and fury
That we look like half-eaten Jell-O men.
We feel like we look,
We taste like we feel.
We battle green leaves and the divine
With our conformist bow-and-arrows
And blood-stained, sinful spears,
But the vineyard,
Where we were once children of the light,
Where cherubs rest and the innocent
Continue to weep,
Is still closed.

Amanda M. Lambdin

Lilacs

A quaint old fashioned flower
Brings a vision back to me,
Of a hillside and a meadow
In the days that used to be.

It is the fragrance of the lilac
How I love its branches too,
For it brings back memories
And the old farm comes into view.

The stillness of the evening
With stars shining high above,
Soft lamp light through a window
And the cooing of a dove.

Purple tones are intermingled
With the moonlight's mystic glow,
And somehow I seem to wander
To the farm of long ago.

Justine Elizabeth Oswald

Fractals

A moss-covered rock acts as miniature mountain range.
Turbulent flows of water,
streams of meandering swirls of bubbles.
Sea waves crashing on rocks jetted upward,
clouds descending in blinding fog.
Thick vapors of darkness, tempest mists,
succeed into colorful forms, spirit endowed hues.

Worlds without end or beginning, scales of time's infinite
Patterns.
Mirrors of light dancing, an endless process, one eternal round.
Holistic intensity, uncertainty of control,
chaining events unpredictable, self-similar interactions.
Built subtle orders of odd limiting beauty expanding,
veiled simple harmony life resonant essence.

Reflective nature, confusion and doubt beneath,
creative truths faceted qualities transformed.
Abstract facts exalted in celestial variety,
approach enlightened kaleidoscope of god-like forms.
Reverent visions of reduced order,
patterns chaos self-organizing immortality.
Invoked emotions, bestowed thoughts.

James Michael Dalton

Since He First Stood

City at night on a hospital bed gasping,
mouthing his melting skyline of stories to the windows, open and
closed, while kids below smoke front coffee shops, wait to
cauterize the tales: to retell them as an elegy.
City drain voices pass through the ancient port, strained of
tradition, ills poured to the ground to seep cobblestone streets,
the smell of decay muzzles the aged walls, quiets the rising
smoke from the concrete fissures, the last efforts of the heart
of a dying man with extended hand.
City exerts a call over itself through the door down the hall,
strains cracking tiles in time with wisps cross town . . .
the urban clash . . . coagulated veins of the man fed and
whispered awake by a prescribed drip, which in turn opens him
his streets, his sewers, his drains, cloudy medicated precision.
He curls toes under sanitized sheets, grasping for the vacuous
ears of those walking 'neath lamplight, stepping over the sores,
steaming those stories . . . his telephone call to the city.
A dying man alone, reaching for the open window's screen,
where the stories catch and whither like the forgotten nets
of the stale old harbor.
A dying man, his tired changing face treated, scribbled,
and tread through youth's ashes, erased into the sidewalk.

Edward Hellenbeck

Rearview Mirror

Saw life passing
like an endless stream
of rushing taillights in the rearview mirror
and a smile came upon my heart.
Warm November opens Indiana sky
as farmland bonfire spews black smoke into black night.

Radio dial glows iridescently
while on the dash sounds of Chrissy, Stevie, Carly
and other she-crooners with masculine affixes
frames our life into some kind of picture.
Sepia-toned, gummed corners hold it in place
in the scrapbook of my mind.

No hurry to get home to life,
I could have driven on in this state forever.
Words unspoken for miles,
a furtive glance yields nothing but thoughts all her own.
I can only imagine
and that's the beauty of it all.

Kenneth Gibson

Dream Lover

Breath of midnight
floats above
while thought, in slumber,
dreams of love.

Scent of loving
fills the mind
when days, with flesh,
are left behind.

Captured kiss
of fancies fall,
as dreaming moment
comes to call.

Joined in wish
the man and maid
where real is not
and dream is played.

With feature fine
though never sure,
In dreams his face
remains obscure.

Kirsten Walker

Ketchup

"They provide everything," she said, and began
to tick off lists: "Blankets, sheets, towels, pillowcases . . ."
rattling on as if she saw her vacation in piles of lines.
"And they stock the refrigerator," she boasted.
"Ketchup, soy sauce, mustard, mayonnaise. . . ."

"And who are they?" I asked in fun.
Me, a person who always tries to take a trip
never quite within grasp, the route slipping away
into uncertainty, a toss-up between bleak and bodacious
with no mitigating squeeze bottle.

It's true I've wanted to explore with Stanley:
hire two hundred bearers with boats
to carry me and creature comforts
into darkest Africa:
writing desk, camp bed, shaving stand, Winchester. . . .

Now a centennial past, I take tamer paths
to shake me with discomfort, if only for a moment
lose my bearings and my sneakered self
in a continent of possibilities;
caught without ketchup.

Gillian Grozier

Life's Turning Pages

Along the river's edge he quietly moves
Dressed in his wading boots.
Though his eyes are dim, he seems to know
Just where the minnows swim.

The net is draped from his aging hands;
A section held tight in his teeth.
His movement is swift, the net is flared.
The bait is no longer adrift.

How tired and weary for a waiting child,
In another time, another age.
But watching him now in his golden years,
Time turns a different page.

These pages of memories keep filling my mind
With moments now held so dear;
No longer the feeling of childhood distaste,
As time moves o'er the years.

Time has a way of changing one's perspective.
If only the child could know,
Events that once seemed unbearably wearisome
Are no longer a tedious woe.

Dottie Riley

Exit, Single File, No Running

So like a parade of colorful clowns,
my encounters with men have been
all moving noisily through bedroom doors
and away to the same tune.

If I dare ask one to stay,
he flashes his grease-paint smile,
hands me a carnation, and
moves more rapidly than the others.

Now I spend more time cleaning,
knowing I'll probably find some souvenir,
memorabilia,
paint-stained handkerchiefs
and dried flowers.

I merely add these to all rest,
piling up too securely,
close
all doors once known
to circuses.

Joyce M. Grosko

Our Industrious Savage

His cobalt language wiggles and boogies
Like a brilliant wet poem.

Slowly grinning and smiling at the
Shlamiels and charming dwarfs of the underworld.

Respect for the mad, white music,
As it fills the dark corners of small rooms.

Winking at women, whose heads move
To the moaning trombone.

Wit and wisdom glowing in his gold mine
And drifting from his melancholic belch when the night is
Through.

He ricochets off earthward friends
And accidentally inspires masterpieces.

Lustfully squinting, gently leering: primitive dreaming
Of things his ignorance has set on pedestals.

Salome Morrow

Monet's Garden

What was it like in Monet's garden?
Through the kitchen, past the larder

Water lilies floated placid
'Tangled light on petals tacit.

Over the bridge to lush of flowers
Stroll in rose-red, blue-green hours.

Where selfish thoughts and meanness faded
On dreamy walks all flicker-shaded.

What was it like in Monet's garden?
When he sketched the history of his ardor

And left his paradisal garden
To the shrine of beauty for all men.

Mary Leonard

The Rock of Ages

I met a rock one day,
The ocean killing itself over inevitability
Each drop an unanswered question
Soaked to the bone
And despite my greeting,
The rock was silent
Gave nothing back
The question I asked was simple
Older than the meaning of the word,
And still I was ignored,
Bloody soul beating against cold stone,
Until finally
My blows were answered.
And as I stood, despairing,
The rock crumbled to sand and was washed away.

Dylan Cunningham

Burn-Off of Light

Toward morning
long low-hanging clouds
spoke mockingly of the dying campfire.
Words poaching slogans
a realm of subconscious programming.

Birds of prey talons stretching out.
Craggy mountain outcropping topping off
in mind to convert a loss.

Down, down, perceptibly a noise.
Though noise would not commit itself
of being nervously pretty
winds began funneling up intentions
up from underneath fire sparks
in light of curl and pinafore.

Could I remember "once upon a time"
conscious of how nighttime spumes
to curb: however else is lost.

Clyde Tressler

The Peripheries of Love

Through waning afternoons we glide
the watery peripheries of love. A silence, a quietude falls.
Above us, the sagging pavilions of clouds.
Below us, rough pebbles slowly worn smooth
grate in the gentle turbulence of yesterday's forgotten
rains.
Later, the moon like a virgin lifts her stricken white face
and the waters rise toward some unfathomable shore.
We sway gently in the wake
of what stirs beneath us, yet leaves us unmoved . . .
curiously motionless, as though twilight might blur
the effects of proximity and distance,
as though love might be near-as near
as a single cupped tear of resilient dew or a long-awaited
face.

Michael Burch

Life Is Like Four Seasons

There are reasons for life's four seasons.
They teach us to live and how to give.
First comes the springtime in your life.
It's the time to grow, which seems forever slow.
You want to be thirteen and then sixteen.
You want to finish school, so you are no longer a little fool.
By the time you are twenty-five you go on to summertime.
You move on to summer when you meet your lover.
You get married, have a family and home which is your own.
To some summer never comes, but to those that it does
How lucky they are to see another season go by.
Now you are fifty and that is so nifty.
"Oh," you say, "autumn time is here,"
And how fast spring and summer disappeared.
Autumn time is to enjoy and get ready for retirement,
Because that is the assignment for this time of the seasons.
Well, I think I did my best and I can sit back and let my
Mind rest.
I'm happy I lived this long and I am ready for winter to come
With a song.
It seems that I just winked, for winter to come so quick.
I am so lucky to still be here and wait for winter's end to come,
Which is very near.

Frances Buratovich

Oikodomoo'mai

At times I am impressed
Not just by the beauty
But also by the suffering of life
And more how the two are faithful
And will never be divorced
Striving together (as two hands knead)
Two guiding, building a life
That speaks of a reality beautiful and real
And things muck like sediments
Whisper into the moorings of our hearts
And quietly describe the secrets that lie there
All the while educating us
Shepherding our eyes
Up to the pastures
Of what is truly beautiful
Hoping for migrant hearts

Kyle Hendrickson

Breezy Freeze

I dip my fingers into melting ice,
Melting Tiger's Blood.
Avalanches sliding down Styrofoam,
Staining mud-pie hands,
And from there, saturating mud-pie strands
Of summer bronze hair that clings
To snow-cone lips, but those were things
That went unnoticed.

My tongue, as its temperature dropped.
The ice
That my spoon knocked off into my lap,
Impossible
To retrieve before melting. My head that
Dropped back, frozen,
Pounding for what seemed like forever,
But passed quickly with laughter.
And my sweaty mud-pie toes
Wiggling outside the car window,
Cooling off in the car's lazy breeze
As I recovered from my summer brain freeze.

Misty Dawn Irving

The Sunrise and Sunset of Life

Her hands flutter about her face
like hummingbirds at play.
Her pale hazel eyes glisten with tears.
Her chin quivers.

Looking at me,
she wants answers,
she needs reassurance,
she seeks comfort.

Lost memories return:
homemade bread, warm cookies,
moist greetings after school,
a haven in her arms.

I'm not ready, Mom.
I need you; I want answers.
When did this happen?
My homework isn't done.

K. Stehr

The Whatchamacallit

Grandma has a problem, and she's given it to me,
She's lost her "Whatchamacallit" and I'm to search and see
If I can find it for her . . . wherever it may be!
She moved the three couch pillows . . . muttering,
"Oh dear! Oh dear! Perhaps it's fallen."
So I look . . . but there is nothing there. . . .
"Just a bit of dust, Grandma," and I rush to find the
Broom. . . .
Grandma is noisily muttering, "It's just got to be in this room."
She's lost her "thingamajigs" and "thingamabobs" a few times
In the past,
But they were kitchen articles and I found them for her fast!
I picked up a Reader's Digest . . . a magazine we both took
And her Doctor's Prescription . . . her "Whatchamacallit" was
Tucked neatly in the book!
Now . . . if her "Whatchamacallit" is lost again,
I'll know just where to look!
(Most of us have a "Whatchamacallit". . . don't you all agree?
My "Whatchamacallit" is my "Elusive Converter"
For my V.C.R./TV.)

Norma Sherk Henderson

Teacup Universe

You live within the seamless, rippled walls
Of porcelain, refined and smoothly white.
A powdering of dust that gently falls
From stale suspension drifting in the light

Has settled on the curves enclosing you,
And undisturbed, it thickens every year
To coat your china kingdom.
Only through the safety of seclusion are you here.

Content to be confined in what you know,
You never look beyond the blank and cold.
But curious and restless, I forego
Your blissful stupor, dead serenity,
And clinging to the rim of painted gold,
I pull myself up over: I am free.

Tabor Elisabeth Skreslet

Rain

Had the sky shed its final tears?
The rhythmic moaning of the sea boded a sad day,
The indignant sun, with an apron of scurrying clouds,
The wind sighing through the trees.
The air heavy with moisture,
Wearily, the heavens burst, emitting her fury,
Pelting rain, pouring down in cascades,
Sweeping, splashing, forming streaming gullies,
Eased of her burdens, she gave way to the brilliant sun,
Smiling victoriously, embracing the world,
Bestowing her light on my white washed village.
Her generous gifts exalted my spirits,
My world gave way,
My world was bathed in infinite beauty.

Ruth Posner

Coloring Pencils

The coloring pencils
Are scattered on the table
Like bright sprinkles
Over melting ice cream.
You want to eat them,
To devour them all.
But, first, you must draw her,
Create her from the rib in your brain,
So she can dance with the moon,
Sit at the table,
Share your ice cream,
Look in your eyes,
Dream with you,
And color your life
With the hues of childhood
And the shades of lust.

Maryela Martinez

The Trains in Paterson

I can hear the trains in Paterson,
That low rhythmic rumbling,
That long lonely whistle blowing, muted.
The air must be thick to make a sound like that, muted.
My grandfather must have heard that sound
When he lived here.
William Carlos Williams must have heard that
Sound when he was still alive,
Thinking of falling leaves and wheelbarrows.
So much depends upon the trains in Paterson.
A million people must hear that sound echo,
It's the sound the soul makes on rainy days.
It's the sound the soul makes on long
Weekends spent alone.
It's the sound the soul makes just before
Love turns to indifference.
There are no stars tonight as twilight fades.
It's going to rain soon,
I can hear the trains in Paterson.

Richard S.Ritsma

untitled

yesterday,
sitting with you
on the curb in front of publix,
your smile made me feel conspicuous
and i ducked my head to be unnoticed.

the day before,
when we held hands
and your arms were too long for mine,
your laughter grinding in my ears
sterile and uncomforting.

somehow,
between the frail pages of my journal,
you've become something that you're not
and i've fallen out of love with the real you.

Heather A. Ratcliff

Mr. Salt

He wears a peacock feather in an old mastic hat
Wearing red lipstick, sucking on a candy cane
He knew the devil intimately, for he wears the mask on his
Right cheek
An open black shirt, crucifix around his neck
Black jeans with a razor in his pocket, boots that look older
Than time.
He looks like he's been around, the world exotic is his smell
Long black and silver hair tied in a ponytail.
He smiles at me, my flesh begins to crawl
He is irritating the passengers on the bus
Passing on his words of wisdom, nobody's listening
Except for me, the words are weird, the language obscure
And the reality of his wisdom hangs heavy upon my heart
The bus stops and he set off, with a tip of his hat
But there's nothing there, for the desert is wide and lonely
And before the bus moves on with its busy, restless people
I look back and he is nowhere in sight.
And I am not surprised.

Carrie Ann Kawa

between

i went today
to therapy
to be reminded
that all this
is so sad

amicable and
intelligent
we fight
giving in
to losing

alone together
we will be
more alone
when we
part

no one
to be mad at
or disappointed with
just lonely
and sad

Alice Mohor

One Day

I love my father still
Despite the cruelty of the past,
The attacks, the scorn.

Much later in our lives, we met again
And seemed to understand and accept.
He shared his home.

And then he fell
In hospital; under anesthesia
He lost his senses, one by one.

At home, while wheelchair bound
And very, very old, he said,
"I have no head;
I used to walk."
He could not understand.

Mara Kirsh

The Road Ahead

It was a cold night
as the little girl stepped outside
with her cardigan on to keep her warm.
She had to find her Dad,
who was a soldier lad,
and tell him the bad men had come
and taken her mum.
She walked all through the night,
till morning dawned so bright.
She could see tents in a field.
She would go there.
Maybe they could spare some food;
anything would taste good.
She would ask them about her dad
and stop feeling so sad.
Her mum always said where there's hope,
no one should sit around and mope.

S. Aitkenhead

Dunny Memoirs

Little sisters sit on the dunny can;
Tiny toes barely touching the floor.
I crouch before her in the lantern light
In the draught from the old dunny door.

Mallee moon glows amid a myriad of stars
'Tis the autumn of 'fifty four.
Whispers of sister's fairy secrets do tell
In the glimmer behind the old dunny door.

'Tis my turn now for the dunny can;
'Jamas drop to the rough stone floor.
Little sister hands me some Sunday mail
Off the hook behind the old dunny door.

Huge huntsman creeps from a crack in the wall;
Creepy crawls 'cross the cold stone floor.
Little sister screams down the garden path;
I fall hobbled at the old dunny door.

Mallee moon glows mid millions of stars
As it did back in 'fifty four.
Whispers of sister's echoed secrets still tell
Behind the ghost of that old dunny door.

Heather Heinicke

Artist's Profile
Michael Dale
Redwood Park, SA, Australia

An immigrant from South Africa in 1974, I spent twenty-three years as a high school teacher in South Australia, married, and have one daughter in Queensland and two grandsons. I enjoy classical music, reading, computing, boating, fishing and speculating in shares and play the piano. I lecture in legal studies at the University of the Third Age, Tea Tree Gully. Poetry to me is like music, in as much as it releases pent-up feelings, and gives one a sense of immortality.

Through the Gate

Rough rusty paint, one time red,
The tractor turns over, trying, trying to start.
Finally a stutter, a cough,
And then welcome black smoke.
Eyes lift from the gauges to the field,
Worry shifting from the tractor
To the harvest.
Bone-cold fog, and worries, is the ground too wet?
Will the price hold? The weather?
Check the hydraulics, feel the motor thrumming
Through the cracked black wheel.
Frosty white breaths from the dog
Trotting alongside, wary eye on the wheels.
Through the gate and into the field,
Into another harvest, another season.
Another worry.

Carol Reiter

Artist's Profile

Rhonda Mohlmann

Kardinya, WA, Australia

This poem was inspired by reflecting on my own experiences, along with those of others whose feelings were similar. Gone are the days of conversation or peaceable relaxation, with those of us who love and care for them, often resulting in loneliness for older generations and stress, heavy on our young, brought about by the pressures of these fast moving times. The world is spinning at a swift pace and our children, riding along with. I was born January 26, 1944 at Perth. I am a host parent to overseas students and an occupation security officer; one of my hobbies is writing poetry and short stories. I hope one day to publish a book of my works.

My Heart Is Young

Why do you turn away?
My heart is young and free,
Take the time to know me,
Truth is what you will see.

Do you think I don't remember?
It seems not long ago,
I thought I had forever,
How was I to know?

I walk the path of autumn
While you still play in spring,
For me awaits the cold of winter,
When in summer you shall sing.

Why do you turn away?
My heart is young and free,
It's simply because we view ourselves
And the world so differently.

Years bring truth and wisdom,
It isn't just by chance,
This change is meant to happen,
To time we all must dance.

Rhonda Mohlmann

Old Trouper

Mirrors to her soul,
Are a faded blue.
Thin snowing hair,
Is all askew.

Those watery eyes,
Weakened by spotlight,
Reminisce fondly, sadly,
Of opening night.

Flower strewn stage,
Hands wild applause,
Many curtain calls,
Crowded stage doors.

Sees beauty vanished,
Heart grows cold,
Once was young,
Now she is old.

Then, "Yes, I am she,"
To herself a laugh,
They do remember,
Signs her autograph.

Dawn M. Bracken

A Summer Evening

The moon rose slowly, throwing a luminous glow across the water.
In the clear night sky, stars gave a beautiful vision
of sparkling diamonds on black velvet, patterned to perfection.

Over-hanging trees created eerie shapes
as they swayed in the soft summer breeze.

The warmth of the evening engulfed her whilst
the lapping water cooled her feet as she danced along the shore.
Out of the darkness the haunting melody of a lone musician
on the crest of the hill above
pierced its way through the silence, carving a sweet
memory of this moment in time upon her heart.
A memory of the carefree summer evenings,
and the free spirit in a child.

Cheryl McManaway

Sixteen

I can still hear it . . .
The patter of her tiny feet on the lino floor.
And her cries of distress whenever she tumbled
To the ground.
I can still smell it . . .
The syrupy, candy-like scent of her soft, little face
And the fresh, vanilla perfume of her hair as it swung gently
Against her cheeks.
I can still taste it . . .
The sugary, over-sweet flavour of her half-eaten ice cream.
And the cold, neglected veggies left untouched on
Her pink, plastic plate.
I can still feel it . . .
Her smooth, rounded face cupped in my hands.
Tickling the tiny, pink toes on her feet
And holding her sticky, lollipopped hands.
But I can no longer see it . . .
And although I can still remember some of it.
She is no longer the innocent, carefree child that I once knew.
Could that be because it was sixteen years ago?

Catherine Flanders

Driftwood

Salt crystallized rough driftwood
stubs my foot
and sand flies swarm
from tide wrack
dark against an off white beach.

Light brazen
from whitened sky
enflames the sea exploding blue
with fiercely translucent
scattered cool fires.

To what end
do tides return
the flotsam of mortality
subversive currents take
this driftwood
while feather light breeze
cools sun hot skin
and eyes half shut
perceive the distance. . . .

Adrian Cedric Rogers

Artist's Profile
Rose McCue
Brisbane, QLD, Australia

This poem is very special to me because it was written for my husband who recently died of an incurable illness. He was the driving force behind much of my writing. His encouragement to submit my works for publication made me realize how great his faith in me was. I would like to dedicate 'Changing Love' to him so that in death he will always be remembered by myself, my children Louise, Claire and Karen and my son-in-law, Philip.

Changing Love

The drool that falls from your mouth
Is a sign that age has taken its toll.
I don't want to remember you like this,
But as a virile handsome man
Who once turned my head and
Made my heart leap at the sound of your voice.
I do not want to see your eyes pleading
To be closed by 'alien' ways
But to see in them the sparkle that once set my body on fire,
Wanting you with all my being.
Your body is frail, your mind sharp,
So much so that you still experience the pangs of love
And the feelings of contentment
That would come with requited love.
I love you as I did when first we met
And I will continue to love you no matter
Till the end of time.
You are precious to me,
Even in your eventide.

Rose McCue

Artist's Profile
Guy Bailey
Mannum, SA, Australia

My parents are Leslie and Judith. My child's name is Jesse. I am a farmer. What is it about ghost stories and forsaken places? Fear seems to come instinctively . . . and instinct is usually quite reliable. Writing "Ever Lost Room," I wondered whether imagination gets the better of us, or knows better than us.

Ever Lost Room

And I opened the door
A chilling draught, like an echo from the past, seemed frightened
And time fled
Faded books, yearning to be read, lined cobwebbed shelves,
And her lonely bed lay waiting
For life was trying
A silent clock longed forlorn on an age stained wall,
And her rocking chair still hoping
Life stirred
A forgotten blouse, cold and torn, on a dust-smothered
Floor, and her ragged doll started crying
For she was lost
A dying portrait watched for the young girl it still dreamt of
She started humming
But life was ending
Her soul's diary calling, ever ghost whispers willed foreboding
And her door closed

Guy Bailey

Sunrise of Kilimanjaro

Ascending Kilimanjaro from air so painfully thin,
I hack out my breath in sharp splinters of ice,
my teeth a constant chattering.
As I gaze up to the starlit sky,
the beam of my miner's lamp
skitters across the icy expanse.
"Will I make it," I hear myself sigh.
"Not far now," are the words of my guide.
Though little comfort they bring
as my marrow is chilled and sliced
by the blade of the merciless wind.
"Just one step at a time," I barely hear him say.
Kimba, my guide now for several days
but who's counting, my brain is numb.
Since midnight I've stumbled in eerie blackness
wishing for dawn to come.
But victory is close at hand;
at sunrise, on the roof of the world I'll stand.

Anna Moore

Nadia, Evening Magic

Run, little girl on the shining sands.
Dance with the wind and the waves
Gather the stars in your small white hands.
Spirit of light and air.
Dance, little girl, time will soon be gone.
Moments like these cannot stay
But for tonight, we too can share
The dream in your eyes, the stars in your hair.

Ann Hastie

Artist's Profile
V. Chamberlain
Penneshaw, SA, Australia

I spent my childhood in the British countryside during the 1920's and 30's loving the wide open spaces and the friendly country people. I worked on farms throughout World War II and continued working with dairy cattle until 1965. Our motto was: 'No matter how short an animal's life, it must enjoy it and know only kindness.' Now times have changed and no one considers the animal's welfare. They must suffer so that mankind may profit and multiply. How sad it is, this thing called 'Progress.'

Then and Now

When I was young we lived on a farm and we were free
To roam the meadows, play on the marsh or beside the sea.
In sun, wind, rain or snow we walked to school each day
And politely greeted everyone we met along the way.
The farmhands worked from dawn to dusk, tilling the fields
Helped by their willing horses, Clydesdales, shire or Suffolk
punch
Harness jingled, sunlight flashed from the polished brass
Cows and sheep cropped contentedly on the sweet green grass
While the hens scratched happily amongst the stubble
The air was pure and clean, until "progress" burst the bubble.
Now I'm old and grey, my grandchildren have grown up.
They take their children by car to school and say
'Don't ever speak to strangers, you might get led astray.'
No gentle giants till the fields, no one calls 'whoa' or 'giddup'
there
Tractors tear and rape the land, combines roar and foul the air
Cows, pigs and sheep stand sadly in their fattening pens
While the eggs we eat come from maimed and tattered battery hens.
Oh well! They are only animals! Factory farming is the modern
way,
So eat your fill, put on weight, breathe the poisoned air.
Shout hooray! We've made progress. But is it right and is it
fair?

V. Chamberlain

Artist's Profile
Tony Moore
Stanmore, NSW, Australia

I was born in Suva (Fiji), I am forty-eight. I attended King's College (Aukland). In 1974 I emigrated to Australia. I was a 1976 Olympic 200 metres quarter-finalist and once held many national and international athletics records. I am a torch bearer in the Australian Olympic Relay. My poetry addresses relationships, alcoholism, drug addiction and other social issues. We have lost our way. Only love will restore us spiritually. We once loved people and used things. Today, we use people and love things. I believe my poems can affect attitudinal change. My wife and I live in Sydney with our three sons. I am a Senior Business Analyst with Qantas Airways.

Spiritual Moondance

Close your eyes while I touch you with breath
Which has come from down deep in my soul.
Feel the love that engulfs you, replenish
To make you as new and as whole.
See the shimmering glow on the water
From the moon's gentle radiant light.
There's a sky sparkling brightly with diamonds,
And a beautiful woman in sight.
It's a marvellous night for a moondance,
And the stereo's playing that song.
I could hold you like this for a lifetime,
Who'd imagine that love was this strong?
Feel the breeze of the night like a whisper,
Blowing kisses through soft flowing hair.
Let my mouth find your lips in a moment,
As we float like a cloud through the air.
It's a scene which will go on forever,
For as long as we're husband and wife.
Kindred spirits meant just for each other,
On this earth now, and in the next life.

Tony Moore

Artist's Profile

Jan Anderson

Charters Towers, QLD, Australia

I have a fascination for the sea and my first and other poems were written there. I lived for some years on the gold coast and now have moved back to Charters Towers. I have always loved the bush where I was born and have now returned. I have written some poetry about the bush inspired by my partner, David, also my daughter, Jodi, who has always encouraged me to do something with my poems. The sea is so peaceful, or emotional, depending on your mood. I wish to share this emotion and beauty with whoever reads my poetry.

The Sea and Me

The sea is a friend when you need one
with a beauty no one can compare
to meet your need for seclusion
you can be sure it will always be there

I feel the magic quite strongly
the pull of the waves and the sea
it seems to be forever calling
with the offer of peace there for me

The cliffs with the rocks far below them
the breaking of waves on the shore
they beckon me onward forever
to peace on this earth evermore

What is it that holds the attraction
and brings me back time and again
to stare at the far blue horizon
and wonder where will it all end

The gulls glide onward forever
on the crest of the waves of the sea
looking for something eternal
a place to be safe and be free

Jan Anderson

Artist's Profile

Judith Walden

Auckland, New Zealand

This poem reflects a need to retain my sense of humour as we all witness the ever-growing influx of imported gewgaws which flood the market with their sheer audacity. I enjoy sharing my writing with friends who understand my need to laugh at the absence of quality and integrity present in today's consumer-based society. My poems, which examined the sense of the ridiculous, offset the more serious poetry I write with a spiritual theme.

Porcelain Cherubs

Occupying their own corner
of fluffy new-age Heaven
next to the deli bar:
$19.95 porcelain cherubs.
White chubby porcelain skin.
The manufactured aging
a charcoal tattoo of
mapmaker's precision gone wrong.
Carefully measured crazing
a century away from
dropped cups and cracked reality.
Chiffon candy floss pink loincloths
and lemon wings
like mass-produced meringues.

I was aghast at their sheer tackiness.
A spontaneous intake of disbelieving breath
my fingers positively itching
to buy one and present it straight-faced
to some unsuspecting friend.

Judith Walden

Artist's Profile
Peter Dane
Russell, New Zealand

I was born in Berlin in 1921, fled to England 1939, married Gabriele in 1945 and graduated in London in 1952. I taught in Uganda and New Zealand, retired to the Bay of New Zealand, then retired to the Bay of Islands in 1998. I have been living on my hobby-horse: learning and teaching. I am also an environmental activist. This poem is for our daughter who, at thirty, died of over-medication in a mental hospital.

Nancy

She was so delicate and light.
'Snowflake'
I sometimes called her.
Slow to walk and slow to talk,
Her slender fingers
Walked eagerly on the piano.
She loved to watch
The intricate patterns
Her brother made
With his Meccano.
She was at home with
Tenuous links,
And as she learned to play
Bach and Chopin
Knew instantly
The intended phrasing.
Summer and autumn
Eluded her.
The snow thawed
In the early spring.

Peter Dane

Cyclone

Monsoon finally makes retreat,
Farms supposed to be filled with golden thread,
Sudden dash of rain, devastated fields.

Forlorn villager waits in rain, in vain,
Eager, wet eyes for relief from nearby neighbors,
Faraway friends, scattered rice, torn wet clothes.

Goddess will descend in mid-October.
This time she will arrive on elephant,
Leave for her husband's home in Kailash on a boat,
Green fields, golden paddy, modest rain, and vermilion red.

Tidal waves, wild angry wind:
Coast guards will flash signals of death.
Death dances, living flesh for city slums,
Bargain body for death.

A skeleton of Goddess waits in silence.
Rain disrobes her heavenly breast.
Teenagers pray, "Give us wealth, beauty, fame."
Women in new wet saris in mid-October say,
"Kill passion, lust, greed, anger.
Kill death, kill hunger."

Mandira Ghosh

Fear

Under the protection of darkness,
In the middle of the night,
They come out in sheets so white.

To a darkened house and defenseless family,
With covered faces is where they'll turn,
In this yard they lift a cross to burn.

A church or school is not a place to meet,
With no meeting place to call their own,
Instead you'll find them in their home.

Here on the steps as they speak,
They stand there proudly, behind the law,
With the police protecting them all.

You will not see them in the daytime,
Proudly walking down the street in sheets,
Without protection of a gun, law or police.

Elizabeth Maria Mazzeo

I, Gladiator

I know the crush of eager soldiers,
children who have not tasted blood.
Faceless enemies unseen and unknown,
young men sense how easy.
Hard is hand to hand with familiars,
companions perhaps,
who must destroy you to live.
You assign them strength and powers
you cannot match, and avoid locking eyes.
Self-doubt and mortal fear intertwine like
snakes, two ways of meaning the same thing.

But it is time. I look down at my bare feet
on the dirt floor of the cell
and jump rhythmically like a Masai.
I make sounds I've never heard.
I pound out mantras of surrender
and invincibility until at last
it is accomplished. In the silence
I can no longer find my terror.
I am ready to kill my friends.

Bart Marshall

Our Dancing Years

We have waltzed in old Vienna, you and I,
Where the lovely notes of Strauss caress the sky
We have tangoed in Paris, to the tune of jealousy
And our fox trot was a beauteous thing to see
In Russia with the Cossacks, we flung our feet out wide
And in Greece we did our version of our British palais glide.
In Spain we danced flamenco though we lacked a lot of rhythm,
And our rumba in Brazil caused a lot of criticism.
With friends we stripped the willow to the beat of Jimmy Shand
And we quick stepped to Glen Miller and his trumpeting big band.
We've danced towards the sunrise with oak leaves in our hair
And we joined the summer solstice and the druids dancing there.
We've danced through life together since we were joined as one
But our knees are now arthritic and our dancing days are done,
But one last dance my darling, one dance for you and me
We will dance the danse macabre to our local cemetery.

Dorothy Beaumont

Artist's Profile
Pam Hill
Blackpool, United Kingdom

I write just as things come into my head. 'Seasons' was written one bleak afternoon. 'Our Grandchildren' I wrote recently, while thinking it is nearly eight years since our daughter lost her second one of the twins at birth. I have many little poems or verses in a book. I just jot them down as they come, and I really just enjoy doing it. I am fifty-four years old and was born in Barrow-in-Furness and am very proud of my town. I am married to Ray and have two daughters, Ruth and Rachael.

Our Grandchildren

I was waiting for a grandchild
When will it be I'd say
Your dad would say don't worry
It won't be far away
Then came your unexpected news
It's twins you were expecting
The time had started going past
But then at three months one you lost
Don't worry we said
It won't happen again
You tried to keep the other in vain
But in the end baby Amy still died
So again with you we sat and cried
Now you have little Emily Rose
A little darling is she
But in our hearts we still believe
That really there should be three.

Pam Hill

Artist's Profile
Norma Keeling
Oadby, Leicestershire, United Kingdom

I have recently retired so that I now have more time for my poetry. I have been married to a gem of a man for forty years, and have three gorgeous daughters and four grandchildren, who are all the loves of my life. I am a very emotional person, and my poetry does reflect this side of my nature.

Senses

As I sit here by the window
My mind is running free
I know there's beauty all around
Although I cannot see

I feel the sun upon my face
The gentle breezes too
The cool refreshing raindrops
The scent of flowers filled with dew

I hear the birds up in the trees
Their chattering never ceases
Sending messages of love and hope
To all God's lovely species

I sense and hear and feel it all
As if it's just for me
Created specially as it is
Because I cannot see

Norma Keeling

The Abandoned Land

The carrion birds
wing over the village,
watching the land below
with unblinking eyes.

The soil crumbles into dust
while all the crops
shrivel sun-scorched black
in the devastated,
desperate, famine land.

Corpse-white cattle bones
surround the frail village
like grim outriders
of the cruel inhuman earth
where the thin, faint
pulse of life
falters and stops
as the starving children
die unprotesting
in the flaming furnace
of the blazing midday sun.

Stephen Gyles

Can I

Can I give you cause for a moment
to re-live the pleasures that we have often shared. . . .
Can I take you to a place where the world around us
no longer exists and it is only you and I and the passion
that is shared between us.
Can I take your hand and guide you to all the hidden places
that are reserved only for your touch.
Can I offer you my body, my soul and my love. . . .
Can I make love to you, not only with the rhapsody of my hips,
but with the wealth of my mind.
Can I give you the freedom to leave my side
while at the same time holding you close to my heart.
Can I entice your lips with the sweetness of my kiss. . . .
Can I close my eyes and envision you here, next to me . . .
Can I love you without needing you
and desire you without shackling you. . . .
Can I feed on your strength without losing my control,
can I be the one you reach for, always. . . .
Can I.

Michelle Halbert

The Old Man and the Plow

Walking
endless walking,
how many hours had he wasted behind a rusty plow?
Just as his father
and his father before him
had lived their lives by the land,
so too was he destined, or was that doomed,
to see out the rest of his days trudging up a windswept field.
He had not been born for this.
Rather, he was born to it.
There had been a time when he longed for more,
when strong young hands grasped at dreams,
but those same hands now grew tired and weak,
the wrinkled products of an age spent by the land.
How many summers, he wondered aloud,
and how many more?

Bree Peterson

The Sound of Trains . . .

Heavy smog filled the airless streets
Everything the sound of trains
A homeless woman sits crying out
The world had passed her by
The socks worn off her feet
While she is torn by hunger
Inside I feel pity
I also pass her by
Within the rest of the world
She had gone unnoticed today

I sit on the dirty pavement
Everything the sound of trains
I feared me, a homeless woman
I cried out, everyone passed me by
While I pretended my heart was broken
Inside I know their compassion
But all passed me by
Within the rest of the city
I got up and walked with the world
Unnoticed today

Dawn Morra

Artist's Profile
Tracey Booth
Rainbow Vic, Australia

Born October 24, 1977, Manchester, England. Parents: Eric and Theresa. Married to Tony Martin. Children: David, Sara. I am writing this poem to show awareness in the area of mental health, as many people are unaware of the problems that are associated with the conditions or simply choose to ignore the signs until it's too late. Please take notice and care about what happens to us.

Manic Depressive

As I sit here with my head tucked beneath my knees,
My hands crossed behind my head,
Rocking backwards and forwards, so are my emotions.
Thoughts of 'Why me?' and 'What did I do?'
Are running through my head.
All I can feel is loneliness and confusion.
The indecisiveness of my brain is thrown
Into turmoil when moods change so quickly.
To not have control over your emotions
And your brain's ability can be a frightening experience.
To weep uncontrollably for no apparent reason
May bewilder and astonish, but manic depression is reason enough.

Tracey Booth

In Cameroon

Orange hair, orange skin, dirty, gritty, in your face, in your
Eyes, in your mind.
I share a seat with a hairy monkey, petit cousin de l'homme,
And bush taxi with a half dozen other mumbo jumbo meat loaf
Wannabes.
The stocky driver secures his moss-green door with a length of
Wire as I wonder what other parts of this multi-colored tin can
Vehicle are similarly attached. A recyclist's dream.
He throws a wicked little grin at me, offering the bench seat
Between himself and the local upholder-of-the-law, a spot that
Will leave me straddling the gear shift. Non, merci.
Trees, trees, village, trees, trees fly past my windowless
Window.
Friends, loves, children, lives, deaths, swirl behind my
Non-seeing eyes.
Then comes the rain, neither a London drizzle nor a friendly
Drip, drop, drop to refresh the summer crops,
But a brilliant crash of reality like Noah's tears upon the land.
Quickly we become entrenched in the burnt sienna mud.
When will I escape this all too physical, all too vibrant
Country, the armpit of Africa?
How long, how long until I'm walking familiar streets,
Cruising the mall, watching CNN?
But then, where's the vibrancy in that? I suppose I'll stay.

K. Medley-Kimber

The Impact of Love

The bride of years sat at her kitchen table
opened her worn Bible, read Psalm Ninety-One.
"Take refuge under his wings," passage
touched her heart.
Vegetable soup simmered on the stove,
almost unnoticed. Gentle fall breeze, entered
via window, caressed her face.
Her thoughts preoccupied with the
doctor's report: Alzheimer's.
Personality changes she'd noticed, irritability,
forgetfulness, self-absorption, withdrawal from
responsibility and social activities.
Yet he was still her youthful groom.
Bringing the coffee cup to her quivering lips,
she felt at one with the cool autumn breeze.
Closing her Bible, she remembered
spoken vows of so many years ago
and arose to take chocolate anniversary
cake from the oven.
Grasped the impact of love: in health, in sickness.

Evelyn Aholt

this is not a love poem

i pause to consider the gravity of my hair
yours had just begun to die when i knew you
fingers trace scars down taut cheek
i caress them lovingly; they remind me of you
i thread my splintered arms close,
closer to where you are not,
prohibiting cold, fear-insulated:
warming, icing, it makes no difference;
you are still gone;
at night I dream in your soft terror,
your lips: shredded agony,
attesting to your ignoble disintegration
"invalid, in-valid," you said
the drip, drip, drip upon sallow cheek;
dull, dull, duller, i saw the evolution
until there was nothing left but dust
to think, they itched to vivisect you,
anxious to begin their learning
for what more have scholars to learn from your beating heart?

Rebecca Gordon

Thunder

You move through me like thunder.
I hear echoes of eternity in your voice
as you whisper my name over and over again.
We are like a storm moving over the ocean,
now raging with violent winds, now quiet in its intensity.
I crossed into what I thought was emptiness
and found myself in your arms, dreaming of things I had never
dared.
I found my feet did not want to run anymore.
My soul was not so restless.
Something in the rhythm of your soul would not let me go.
It caught me with its haunting chords and left me wanting more.
I sleep and I dream vivid dreams of bursting colors,
the colors of our souls.
Flashing red burns the blackness;
blue and blue fades to silver and silver to white.
And there we are . . .
when there is nothing left of us but heat,
the energy burned from us in war or passion or both.
When we go beyond ourselves and become a little more of the
other.
Who are we then? Gods . . .
for an infinite moment . . .
we know what it feels like to be worshipped.

Barbara Martin

Morning

I always wanna smile
when I wake up
with you in my bed
in the morning
Wanna smile and shout
from every mountain top
how much I wish
For morning
to find us again
and again, and again . . .

Sierra Leone Joyce

On the Train

In the odd light of the train car
I see men bundled against the cold
The black woolen caps are tightly pressed
On stubborn or yielding heads alike,
And rough woolen scarves are poised
As shields against the rough Long Island wind.

These men have had a long day.
The New York winter has played a trick.
This is Buffalo weather, kid!
Can you take it?

I think of huddled masses
Yearning to breath free.
I think of quiet desperation.

Doors open and they rush
Into the cold and blustery night.
To me, each one a volume,
A unique tale of mystery.

I'd like to remove each woolen cap
And search for mind prints.
I need to read them all.

Dianne Honig

Out by the Garden Gate

Children, I forgot to tell you
When I left the other day
That I was meeting a friend
Out by the garden gate.
Our meeting was so friendly
I decided to stay
So don't fret or cry for me
I am as happy as I can be.
I asked my friend to tell you
I don't suffer pain anymore
For this friend of mine is Jesus
And He is always right by the door
If you hear Him knocking
Please open the door and let Him in
He can give you peace and comfort
And He can be your Best Friend.
Put your arms around each other
"A smile upon your face"
I am just standing here with Jesus
Out by the garden gate.

Kate Blount

Closeness of Strangers

An elegy for John Henry

Night poured in slickly through a crack in the skyline,
    Soaking the city; ink spilling on a blotter.
Having stepped from one blackness into another,
    I go in search of hospital elevators.
Faceless voices drift past in shadows of despair.
Leaving the brightness of the lift, I find his room.
Pausing at the open door, my eyes seek him out.
    In bilious green light, reluctantly bleeding
    From a bank of monitors beside his sickbed,
He's barely discernible; pillow-propped, in pain.
With a voice like dead leaves scudding across concrete,
He greets me with the question: 'Is that you, my son?'
    Walking over to the bed, I reach for his hand
    To grip what feels like a bundle of cool, dry twigs.
    In silence, we waited in the semi-darkness.
I had come twelve-hundred miles, not to watch him die
    But just to be there, with him, so he'd know I cared.
Love him? I didn't know him well enough to say.
Death stole into the room and departed, with Dad,
    Leaving me alone. But with Dad, I always was.

David J. McGrattan

Toto Corde

Tonight I gazed into the eyes
Of Phosphor, and touched the
Moon's Mandorla sunflowers face.
For an eternity has ego feasted
On the canker of the white
Rose and slumbered on a Flynt
Bed of singing advent
Daffodils; making April
Of my December vision. At
Lazar's death, Kristos
Wept; toto cordo, flos Matris
Virginis; placate with
Song a darkened heart:
A gramma of passion sans a
Tear. Faltering, a kernel
Lingers with that greens not,
Searches the will; seeking
Forever the glance it seeks;
Words once spoken roar silent:
Arid August now and ever.

Ken Stallings

Making Memories

Today I helped you with a button
As your hands no longer flex and bend
And, while walking today, I gave you my arm
To lean on because of a slight stumble.

We laughed and talked and told each other
Of secret dreams we'd never share.
You gave me insights on becoming older,
And I made you laugh with childish abandon.

We've shared the passing of the seasons
With me being dependent on you.
And, as the months have turned into years,
You now trusting as a child; and I, strong as the parent.

As the days continue to slide by
I enjoy the time we spend together;
The touch of your hand, the sound of your voice;
And, I cherish the memories we have made.

I look forward to sharing each day with you.
The time from the warmth of the morning sun;
To that of the beauty of the nightly moon.
As we spend, hour upon hour, making memories!

Virginia R. Giorgis

On the Ocean Side of Melanoma Road

The waves, they roll gently, and caress the sand,
But not as softly as your hand,
As we lay hidden there in the dunes.
Your touch is leaving me in ruins.
We're on the ocean side of Melanoma Road,
Where I'm losing my vision; I'm in a glaucoma mode,
While wading the river and walking tidal flats,
As we ignore the reality with the idleness of chat.
There is a storm that rages out to sea
As I shuffle through the discards of this life's debris,
And the lightning sears, illuminating my pain,
As our brown skin is kissed by the gentle rain.
Grey cumulous clouds, they bump and they grind,
Stirred to turmoil by the thermals of my mind,
As I'm lost to the depths, the colour of your eyes,
And drown beneath their surface of self-deluding lies.
Overhead, the trees are stirred by the winds of time,
And I close my eyes to the sand storms of my mind,
And wonder about our defenses and what fears wield the trowel,
As I lie here, naked, upon the fortress of my towel.

Ron Peters

Cyclone

It filters through the rank of palms,
staring down the beach.
A cool lick of the skin,
relieving sweat for a moment,
it escapes as quickly as it came.

Nature's caution of the commotion to come.
The air sucks and pops with saturation;
steamy black clouds hang heavy in the sky.
The breeze is elevated;
the palms swing in agreement
to the tune of what is brewing.

Thunder rolls across the waves, warning.
Hurtling up the beach,
a ferocious blast of wind smacks the palms.
They bend to near snapping.
Innocent granules of sand are lifted.
Waves teeter high, then topple.

Cyclone season has begun.

Erin Mould

Artist's Profile
Jane Faire
Fakenham, NO, United Kingdom

I do not write much poetry, if that is what it is, and, to me, it is a very private affair only to be shared with complete strangers! I have a very English garden, which is my greatest relaxation. My father loved his garden as did my grandmother, who insisted on being buried on the side of the church nearest her beloved plot. In my great-grandfather's diary I read, "Sept 13, 1883. Wrought in the Garden." One of many references. He was born in 1801. Links are very real.

The Gardener

Fingers in the soil
The damp earth rich and dark and warm.
Leaf mold aged to a ripe maturity;
Sun stirred fresh rising smells, pervading the air.

Solitary but not alone,
Birdsong and small creatures of the land
Ever present.
Land tilled for a thousand years or more
By the hand of man.

Tangible evidence surfaces;
A green marble, a glass stopper
Faded and opaque with age.
Fragments of pottery, colors bright as new.
Stems of clay pipes, discarded long ago
And endless bits of iron and shell and bone.

Links in the chain of time
We all stand here.
Practical people, similar thoughts,
Watching the emerging shoot
And marvelling at the wonder of it all.

Jane Faire

The Jacaranda Tree

I came to my vehicle tired,
But was blessed with flowers,
Lovely, soft, mauve petals,
Tiny, bell-shaped trumpets,
Like confetti on the car and all around,
Carpeting the paving and the weary moments
Of a long, hard day at work.
My step lightened; I thought, how lucky I am,
So privileged on this last day of spring
To be showered with the joy of flowers,
Gentle little fluted bells, cheering me on my way,
Compelling me to count my blessings.
Hundreds of them forming a soft-hued cover,
Comforting me.
I drove homeward, uplifted,
The wind circling the "blessings"
Up and over the windshield, flying around me!
Some catch in the wipers.
Perhaps remaining to remind me,
Be thankful in life's difficulties.

Maureen Capps

The Last Reveille

The trumpet calls for one and all
To leave their beds of clay and soil,
And watery graves in ocean deep,
Or fields of war where heroes sleep.
Though not to labor as before,
But to new life forevermore.
All work is done, each battle won.
The reign of peace has fully come.
Let ransomed souls rejoice and say,
This is the resurrection day!

Violet E. Slarke

Artist's Profile

J. Bennett

Kent, KE, United Kingdom

My poem is dedicated to all the people who have experienced unrequited love, who have felt that they have to keep their feelings a secret due to a fear of rejection and a need for an uncomplicated life. Specifically, I dedicate the poem to my sister, Caroline, who is always there to help me through every failed relationship and is always supportive of my poetry. Obviously not forgetting my mum and dad and the rest of my family and friends. I love you all, that I will admit.

Secrets

I never told you
But sometimes I go to the top of a hill
And think of the ways you make me feel.

I never told you
That sometimes at night I stare up at the stars
And remember the way you fade my scars.

I never told
That sometimes at night in the pale moonlight
I cuddle the teddy you gave me real tight.

I never told you
That often at night I dream of you
And I'm always hoping you dream of me too.

I never told you
Because when the day comes and I see you again
I look in your eyes and what I see is a friend.

I never told you about the hill,
I never told you and I never will.

J. Bennett

The Scholar

They smiled.
And whispered my name
As if there were secrets
Adults could never understand.
They wiped my nose,
And gave me brilliant crayons
To make my mark
On virgin plains of endless paper.

We sang.
We danced, we played
Those laughing finger-games.
We were a tribe or merry elves,
Cavorting in yet another
Undiscovered Shangri-la!
And after those innumerable naps,
The strange foods;
The presentation of those ornate certificates;
We were advised
That we were now prepared,
For kindergarten.

Donald L. Ransom

Silver Serpent Ring

He said my ring,
simply silver curving around my thumb,
looked like a serpent.
Yes, he confirmed to himself, a serpent,
one that is female and constricts,
pushing life away,
one that strangles him.
Yes, he said, it is the all-powerful female essence
choking him.
And I, as I walked away from him, said
the ring turns my finger green,
and his eyes lit up like I had goosed him,
but then I said,
it's all I have of my grandmother,
this simple silver ring that curves
around my thumb,
skin on corrosive metal
adheres to me,
and I can feel her entrance to my body there,
so she can be free to swim in my veins.

Jennifer Phillips

Artist's Profile
Edi Johnson
Tifton, GA, USA

The operational intelligence of this world that scientists, doctors, and philosophers only discover a little about and give all sorts of names: nature, biology, all ologies, really is actually Cosmic Mind that is "Extra-Terrestrial." We neither possess or control it. Poetry puts me in touch with that mind with God, I believe. Thanks for publishing "Spring Dying."

Spring Dying

My mother died on the seventeenth of April,
and ever since that springtime loss
out of strained rainbow coats of piety,
there's this silver leaf I keep trying to glimpse.
It's back of a dark cloud flying up out of night
like the idea of sunrise must surely have flown
to shatter God's gloom and make him think, "Children!"

To know divine love, it must be sought, must come to rest
Along the cave mysteries of hearts,
Which are clouds' realities; vague kindness of sight
that shields us from startling days
of watching earth loves arrive, then go.

And this silver leaf trembles awhile, then flies
up from stains on every church glass
framing wind and marrow of spirit in us,
some hope that blossoming will grow out of rain
of Aprils when all those light, green things
seem touched by death, somehow, for me
since she left me bereft at that deadly spring.

Edi Johnson

Grace under Fire

Windswept mountains ablaze in the eyes
Of the beholder whose repose lies shaken.

She comforts in the breeze of clouds above
A slumbering sun with haze of red
And glowing amber to laugh,
Until darkness claims her night.

Pure white lilies are her cheeks and
Soft rose petals her smiling lips to hide
That which the rain disturbed,
And no kind word would calm.

She lies beleaguered now as fallen leaf
With radiant color which cannot stand alone
Again 'midst sweet melody of dove and sky.

Her eyes, their color, her tongue, its song
Combine to part the smokey shroud as
Soft-winged words rise to Heaven's throng.

Windswept mountains ablaze in the eyes
Of the beholder whose repose lies shaken.

She will not be won.

Kemarie Ann Campbell

Post-Apocalyptic Dream Boy

The freak shows of selective photographic telescopic
Connections return
Echoing the wiry old truths and I again invent someone new
A flicker of hands, a flutter of eyelids; no fixation here,
I hesitate
A wide screen imitation is perfectly cold, but a fully
Automatic air-conditioned consistency requires concentration
Consumed by cravings and death blows
It appears I have already killed him
And my sun eyes still find no east or west
You can come as you are paid, as you go; so gather me up now
In your long arms, your electronic, systematic, mechanical arms
There is no looking glass here, so bring your own miracles
The voice on the telephone, you ask, and the voice says
I am blind
The quiet ascent and descent of space in your buoyant eyes
Would never agree
Looking for you and finding the flow is an art
Silently tuning into the simple lifting and falling of shadows
Only then could we smile
Dreams and nightmares could not harass and I would sleep
Exhausted but safe in your burnt-out Icarus arm

Noeleen Hern

Artist's Profile
Sarah Powell
West Sussex, WE, United Kingdom

"Kew Gardens 1945" is one of the poems in a collection, "Dance to the Caprices of Time," which I recently submitted in partial fulfillment of the degree of M.A. in Creative Writing. The poems explore my family history and immortalize our collective memories. "Kew Gardens 1945" commemorates my maternal grandparents' relationship. The attraction began when they both worked for Phillips Map Making Company. Their first date was the result of a bizarre bet, which led to a loving and lifelong marriage.

Kew Gardens, 1945

Zoom in: A sepia afternoon in Acton, 1918.
Closer: A sly, golden sun slants through dust in an office.
A desk, a box of staples, a black Bakelite telephone,
A woman in beige.
Press your nose to the glass, wipe a circle, listen;
The husky clack of typewriter keys, the phone ringing,
The creak of leather as the woman turns, a girl really,
No more than sixteen, and answers the phone in a shrill tone.
Focus on a man, slightly older, at a drawing board,
A cartographer; he's not looking at his map; his attention's
On the girl's seamed stockings, her legs crossing and uncrossing.
He spies on the play of light in her hair: melted lemon-drops
tied in knots at her neck; the curl of her fingers 'round the
Cord; The way her brow furrows, her lips part.
Crawl in through the back door, push him,
And he'll tell you he's bet a shilling
To ask her to the pictures; it's not the money.
He loves her, even though she earns more than him.
Zoom out: Have a break, a holiday.
Two world wars away they sit stoically at Kew,
Finishing each others' words in a caring but brittle way;
Until the sentences run dry, her lemon-drop hair turns grey.

Sarah Powell

Tuscan Passage

When I saw you last, working in your studio,
Touching furniture, caressing it, loving it, all periods
You could make it, duplicate it with amazing credibility
But it was nothing for you, with your arm sweeping upward
You would grandly say, "It is done, E finito!
In my head it is finished, you must learn this!"

"Taste," he said, "drink," he said, and I did
Learning each time a flavor and aroma, learning each time a
Sensation new and unique, teaching me and those around you
We ate bread, hard and crusty
We drank wine, red and white
We dined as many did before us, communion of all mankind

An experience so simple, but you, my teacher, made it special
Talking philosophy, music, art,
But mostly about the senses, the feeling about things
What is in the heart, body, senses and beyond the spirit
The spirit of Brunelleschi, Bramante, and Ghiberti's doors
"Gates of Paradise," Michaelangelo once said of them
Lucca, town of my heart, Tuscan hillsides alive in my veins
Sadly mourns my brother, my friend, my teacher, who lives no more

Anthony Massaro

Distressful Reminiscence

A sweet smelling mirage wallpapers my eyes
A collage of dreams murals my mind
when I met you, I thought love
was finally smiling upon me
but it was only having another good laugh
Stick some daisies between my toes
and walk me to my room
painted half purple, half blue
and the days produced their hope
as they always have
but I don't know whether to laugh or to cower
I seemed to have misplaced my tambourine
Still, an incredible desire feeds inside my heart's imagination
always reaching, reaching
always slipping, slipping
trying to sleep the pain away
then only missing the point
So I hope you find your love underneath that rock
if not, check the sky's moonlit shroud
My name will be written there in the clouds

Leia McCumber

Just a Pup to Me
Dedicated to Bud Dawson

"He came out of the 60's, walked through three decades
just to say to me, "The truth, I want the truth,
before it's too late, before I die, you must tell the truth
to me."
And I sat looking beyond thirty years,
I saw the jowls lessen, the lines decrease,
the hair turn dark and thick, the expression soften,
the eyes begin to twinkle,
I saw the bloom, and I could have said
something smart like, "The truth! You can't handle the truth!"
or "What is truth? A word! And what is a word? A puff of air!"
But instead I said, "I can see that you're bigger,
and I know that you've grown older,
but what looks like an old man to
the rest of the world is still a flower
child, just a pup to me."
And I led my friend by the hand to the garden
to show him one red bloom.
I said, "It arrives every spring. It reminds me of you."
To which he asked, "Is that the truth?"
I answered, "It is to me."

Marianne Beasley

Aye! The Eye on Sanctity

Bernadette stepped into the hallowed halls of the church
built by the Catholic missionaries, wearing her native
African garb after spending the night with her virile lover,
unprotected by the bonds of betrothal and marriage.

Inside the sacred walls of the gothic cathedral, a solemn
air preserved her reveries of her beloved Justin as he had
smiled at her before her early-morning departure.
She remembered how she had finally found refuge from
among the squalor, depravity, ridicule, and aimless chatter
of the villagers as he approached the altar and genuflected
with a reverence and pious obedience seldom witnessed.

What she could perceive was how the oracles had possessed
the angelic voices of the choir boys whose voices spiraled
upward toward the ceiling as she daydreamed of frolicking
in the opened fields and dancing with joy as she held Justin's
hands. She fervently prayed for a stronger connection to
disturbing thunderstorms, nature, fallen leaves, and rivers.
When the priest drank from the chalice, she waited for
redemption from God so evident in every atom of her existence.

Cecil Williams

Contentment

I had overeaten.
So I reached inside myself and pulled
Up whatever could be pulled up
With what strength I could muster up.
I labored long and hard and
Brought forth snowcapped mountains
And the tallest pines with cones intact
And sparkling stars draped with clouds
And songbirds with half-sung melodies
Resting on their beaks and butterflies
With magnificent wings, extended
And poised for flight, and rainbows
Capturing the essence of promises.
I wept, not due to any emptiness,
But due to the incredible beauty
Of the lone rose that rested
Just out of my reach so that it
Remained in my innermost parts.
I was spent but at peace.

Mary Scott

Dispersing Memories

With gold-trimmed edge, a teapot, cup, and saucer
was your first gift to me; was all you could afford to offer.
Then later, as we kissed and walked by the sea,
a piece of driftwood you carried home and gave to me.
Letters of "I love you" you often wrote,
a hastily scrawled "I can't live without you!" note.
Fond memories of love and sweet, shared laughter,
we planned our future, our dreams of forever after.
The years swept by, they multiplied, we prospered;
children came, our love we fortified.
Homes, three cars, a boat, investments; all superfluous security
against the winds of change; those mysterious billows of enmity.
The scourge of love, an adulterous heart,
those precious dreams will scatter and depart.
A lesson sad, so late in life to learn,
as one by one each fond memory I throw away or burn.

Annette Akerman

Silver

If I were swayed . . .

To the magic tempo,
I might write it out feverishly
Or keep it to myself,
Then spew it out suddenly,
Like the water in a whale.
I don't think I'd suffer as
Much: I would know to rely on
The words as my cable, keeping
The bungee jumper safely in
The surreal sky. Silver has
Always been kind, I think, and
For one reason or for another
I feel weak. Weak enough
To drop a consonant here,
A syllable there.
Because it is me.

Joel Nelson

Alter Et Omnia

We see our neighbours in the queue
In unaccustomed vacuum, wondering.

The singles study the couples,
Slyly amused at the wedding rings.
How do they endure the relentless companionship,
The erosion of dirty laundry and breakfast cereal,
Joint bank account, holidays, public face, in-laws?
What joy in each others' bodies
With unwanted hair and removable extras?

The attached consider the singletons,
Momentarily pitying their silence.
How can they maintain a solitary mastery
Over car keys, tax returns, shopping lists, dental appointments,
The anarchy of life's infrastructure of survival?
No familiar touchstone of opinion,
And ever uncertain physical attraction.

We shuffle forward, easily distracted,
Never reckoning the glories shared
Of the freedom of dreams and fires of genius
And wild, wild passion in bluebell woods.

J. E. Acheson

Artist's Profile
Julia A. Vogel
Nassau, NY, USA

Poetry has always been my outlet to help me to express my feelings. Whenever I write a poem I understand why I needed to write that particular poem. This poem is really about my mother and it was written after her death on February 23, 1998. This poem encapsulates my feelings about my mother and my family. I'm sure that others have had similar feelings and hopefully will be able to understand my poem and be able to understand that they are not alone.

The Mantel Clock

The mantel clock sees all, knows all,
and yet is silent
like my mother was during her illness.
It stands watch over the family
a silent guardian in its dark wood housing.
It is the face of time and yet also the faces of my family,
and all those who have ever seen it
are reflected in its silent gaze.
It holds those faces and those lives and protects them.
It is ever faithful in its role,
never wavering,
always steady, always silent.
It wasn't always silent.
Many years ago my father wound it,
and it chimed its low, deep sound.
But over time it has been neglected,
and no one bothered to wind it anymore.
So it sat, gathering dust,
but never forgetting the days when it could chime;
never forgetting the memories it contains.

Julia A. Vogel

Lovebug Lore

Lo, amber-poled drift 'way,
Scurried 'long hot, late-summer breezes.
Quite peculiar, though, these they are,
And lead to question reason.

Black as pitch 'tween these crowns of amber,
Imbued by melancholy oneness.
'Tis naught sublime to be they are,
Whilst death ebbed a life: the treason.

And now he hangs till glory wind
Could try decouple pang,
Though mercurial gusts shall blow them far
Her trail remains the same.

She dies, ascribed, dead-season.

David Eric Thomas

Vessels

They are vessels,
navigating silently through the sometimes murky and rough,
often calm and still waters of life.
They are strangers.
Though most seem strong and withstanding,
I wonder about weaknesses that have been repaired
and holes that have been patched.
Many are plain and simple,
but they hold secrets of outlandish exploits
and surprising adventures.
A few are gaudy and bold,
but their contents are unnecessary or destructive.
Some drag cargo they long ago meant to purge,
while others carry riches unseen by the passing outsider.
They are vessels transporting stories and memories,
hopes, desires, and dreams for the journey.
Though we share the waterways from one port to the next,
they are strangers.
We unintentionally touch,
and they are strangers still.

Elizabeth Stoeckel

damn! my glasses. . . .

she's not quite sure, if there's a god or
not; still, she never fails to blame her
problems on jesus. . . .

wan'dring down the hallway
smashed glasses on the floor
a sea of faceless people
blurred numbers on the door
voices wash by, misty
float, stagnant, in the air
vague shapes and shoes and outlines
but no one's really there
through deserted places
you plow on through the crowd
souls and minds are empty
but still extremely loud

she lost her glasses that day
but for the first time in her life,
things seemed most definitely clear. . . .

Cory Choy

One Small Acre

In a dim time alone she stood,
a stranger of the neighborhood.
The fear of a past alone did take her,
in her mind's eye saw one small acre.
Remembering again the child she lost,
living the pain at her heart's cost.
Another mother that had to raise her,
a glimpse of hope in one small acre.
Working against the hands of time,
her soul she lost to make a dime.
Someone she loved that did forsake her
enforced the dream of one small acre.
Giving all that there was to give,
slowly dwindled the will to live.
With sweat and blood and pain to break her,
Heaven's light shown on one small acre.
Finally the dream was in her hand,
the deed belonging to the promised land.
Her hands now shook and pain did take her,
she gave up life for one small acre.
The young girl viewed the headstone round;
tears flowed like rain and watered the ground.
For years she searched and tried to reach her,
a mother's love found, on one small acre.

Joseph D. Neloff

this night closes around me

this night, hollow as it seems
brings me pictures,
images of shadowy dreams
lay in motion through
lamplight pools of the moon,
and mist surrounds
a blanket of cool gray wrapping . . .
there's solace found in this night,
its maudlin scene plays
to fear in its ending,
my heart,
heavy in comfort,
dark with pride and strengths
from unknown sources
too often masked by light
and dancing sun-made shadows deceiving,
but in this night, close around me,
a vision persists,
an unseen clarity for my soul.

Damon Bembry

read all about it

i still smell newspaper print on my fingers
acrid and burning in my nostrils; burning,
singeing the skin. the words it once spelled
out blurred and smudged by my own tears and
sweat, proclaiming my insecurities, open for
all to read and judge on the front page.
i have to get rid of these!
get rid of my simplistic inhibitions . . .
i'll swallow them. savoring the ink on my
tongue, it rids me of my fears.
nothing satisfies my tastebuds better than
the taste of safety from abandonment.
black esophagus, cleared soul . . . i thought.
ink corrodes intestines, i don't feel pain,
i'm safe, no one knows . . . me.
can't move my lips anymore, want the
tears to come, only ink flows from eyes.
want to feel . . . anything. bloodstream
flows ink now. cannot feel. cannot live.
cannot love. love me so I can love. . . .

Roxanne Lynn Heaney

Clockwise

Hands circle around One rivet
Circumscribing Seconds, not Firsts
Aging along a disk, progress delineated
What type?

Sixty equals Zero, a Whole
Twelve, both start and finish
Hands name the meaning
If they are beginning or ending

Ashley Pendergast

First at the Edinburgh Royal Scottish Museum

Shifting from foot to black Mary-Janed foot
in the marbled entry all of the exhibits
I listened to words roll out of the guide's coral lisped mouth
as I leaned over dusty lily pads.
it was there I fell for the trick of them in water
at seven years old:
I thought they were drowning
and kneeled in white tights
to give my air
though they fled from offered bubbles
in a most unmarching manner
to the darkness of the fountain flora
before fatherly hands
hauled my soaked head
straight away from the manicured pond
into the stuffed bird exhibit
replete with the hypothetical stuffed dodo
that couldn't have evolved from them
that dippy winged wonder could never fly so free
as dorsal fins give to them silent floating liberation.

Caitlin Steele

Longing

I view the darkness before beginning work.
Daylight will be here soon.
Minute reflections from the street light
glisten in tiny puddles.

My heart is lonely,
like a figure in the rain by a lamppost,
alone,
looking,
longing,
waiting for someone or something.

Like a man in an old black and white movie,
post-war Vienna
or London at night,
lingering for an expected rendezvous.

Being a real man, I am uncertain.
Old answers produce too easily chosen
solutions that fail to satisfy,
like a man who drinks and is still thirsty.
It will be better, I tell myself.
This is only the waiting and the longing.

Thomas Hogan

On My First Visit to the Library

When I first walked into the library
and saw all the books
standing with their backs turned
I did not wish to intrude
I was nudged forth
to make friends
Balancing upon my toes like a ballerina
I pulled a book down off the shelf
and opened it
Sat down
Intrigued
as it chatted on forever
about its adventures

Franco Holmes

Chick's Voice

Team spirit broke for a streak
when his breath ceased
as we, his loyal fans,
withdrew from the game.
Recalling timber in his voice,
shadowing hoops and bounds,
city pride soared
as his team paraded
on common streets. He lead them on
to victory, hearts' dreams made real.
Chick, go now, go
hold a seat for humanity
as we await your calling,
shouting for the winner,
the King himself.
You announce each step
to the final second.
Peace be upon your lips
as our listening souls
hear your everlasting voice.

Deborah A. Johnson

The Actor

I am a stranger,
A painted, flawless face.
A pretender, an imposter
Invented by another.

Lost in a character, never
Knowing true love, true happiness
Or true sorrow.

Sadness strikes my soul
Like a forceful blow of lightning.
How did I let this happen?

Lights, camera, action are
The three words I truly know.
I am an actor, lost in . . .
Another's soul.

Jivonne W. Prioleau-Green

at play

curl your fingers around my waist
stroke the small of my back as I pass
moving, brushing lips
almost the quiet fun we had
attaching bitten-off gummy bear parts
glances like fruit-flavoured sugar
the sticky fingers making window prints
and those fumbling thumb wars

this fun, changing courtship we cherish
expands and contracts, a breathing lung
and a favourite pastime has become
watching pupils grow
feeling that belly button lightning
fire spreading inward and throughout
as your tongue finds me in the dark
sweetly giving puppy licks

Jennifer Joanne Lau

The Old Woman

I see an old woman in the park
playing hopscotch

Her fragile figure
leaping in a joyous pleasure

Her mind is flying . . .
while her body barely clears
the fluorescent lines upon the concrete surface

A reverie I've never appreciated
her smile expresses a pleasure
I've never known.

Does she live life to the fullest
or
do I selfishly expect more

Norma Abrego

Restoration

The touch-up paint doesn't quite match.
It's darker, maybe not as faded,
Perhaps not mixed quite right.
Although I brought it back not once
But twice; I wanted it perfect.
Two men behind the counter.
Exaggerated patience as they explained
It's a formula! There's no room for error.
They catch each other's eye . . . Women.
I don't explain that I'm rearranging,
Starting over in the same place.
Trying to cover holes and markings,
Scars left behind from the life before.
Two minus one.
Again I try to blend the paint, the old and the new.
It's still too obvious, I think.
Everyone will know; they'll be able to tell,
To see it isn't perfect.
I catch sight of my face in the mirror.
The touch-up paint doesn't quite match.

Celeste Cacaci

Heat Wave

Bodies on park benches
covered with wet, white shrouds
Lazaruses resurrected by the setting sun
creep back to dark wombs
whose dead bolts define their lives
On Fifth Avenue, Lexington, and 43rd
asphalt cracks, melts, oozes
What monsters stir
beneath the alligator skin?
What creature will emerge
from this well-incubated egg?
The carapace of metal plates
erupts on Brooklyn Bridge's face
stegosaurus waking from an icy hibernation
or enchanted sleep interrupted
by the smoldering lips of a solar prince?
While dark windows gape
at a city without power, I ask
What will become of us
so fragile in our fleshly shells?

Jerri Lejeune

untitled

they've seen me
toss my hair
into the wind and
smile deeply while
pushing my sun-
glasses closer to my head.

pour a martini
push a smile
deeply into the wind
while tossing
my hair
closer to my head. sun-
glasses
pouring martinis into
small
white paper cups
and
drinks
with a precision grace.

Tyrone Pearce

Promises

Your mouth was a fountain of empty promises.
I drank your words in.
I was weak, and they gave me substance,
but they didn't fill me.
They were like sugar on my burning tongue.
They melted away, leaving me nothing.
The words you spoke with the lips I kissed
turned into ghosts that haunt the cobwebs
in the shadows of my mind.
Your tongue, once so soft and warm,
turned into a viper's tongue,
slashing at my ignorant heart.
Now, my mouth lies silent.
The tears in my eyes do all the talking you'll need.

Tracey R. Grimm

out of

naked belly to the only star out,
laid flat in roof embrace.
the morning night covers like black cotton,
a pillow and clouds . . .
clouds that smother the leafless tree limb,
scrawling poetry on gray shingles.
i am without sleep, but under the sky's dream.
and the air sticks to skin and is humid,
breathes into my hair.
ready to die? it would silence me.
i would miss this wind that flows
black ink onto spacey white,
gathers remaining stars in sallow regression,
pins them onto this night.
this morning blanket that hovers
flies the eyes out of lament.

Jessie Sobey

The Lounge

I perch atop a pile of phone books
stacked in a cracked leather chair.
I smoke thick brown cigars and sip sherry
with weathered, worldly men.
They pinch my cheeks and giggle in my drink.
Fathers approach and speak of their daughters.
I cradle their heads as they cry over
skinned knees and long-ago loves.
I cry too, for those memories I have never known.
Responsibility wore holes in the soles of my shoes
before they could be bronzed.
I smile and politely decline another.

Liz Hein

time

against the grain
love poems are burnt in heaps
and flower beds are constructed
to commemorate the absence of presence
of all thought of every thought of you
but I forgot to remember the thing I hated
when you fell in flower beds
and I covered you with the last
black rose deconstructed dreams devour
the glossy retinas of the past twenty years
when life was the end of all struggle
and deviants became all worth saving
but you forgot to remember the end of the last time
but all of them were the beginnings
when alarm clocks put babies to sleep
in yellow rooms filled with cigarette smoke
exhaled fumes and the clanks of scales
reflected your absence of color
in plastic teething toys
drenched in my snot choking on the end of all beginnings

Cybil Lee Weigel

Anticipation

Cool early breezes and gulls' cries,
Salty sea vapors permeate the air,
A steaming cup of latté, freshly brewed,
Lending its aroma.
No one else yet stirring,
A time of quiet joy and anticipation.

Soon my anxious feeling will take me
Up the narrow path to the rocky heights.
Soon my whole being will be in tune
With rising sun and sparkling ocean
Yielding sights of rarest splendor,
My fervent quest to capture the essence,
The mystic wonder of heavenly hues,
Create a magical scene of beauty with bright yellows,
Pearly pinks and diaphanous blues
Emerging from the drowsy grayness.

Quickly I dress, taking up my canvas bag
Of paints and brushes and small arches block,
Inspired and eager for the challenge.

Mary L. Barrett

Fear

I saw fear once
it was a pale yellow
like a faded poster.
I knew it was there
from miles away
by the smell of sweat and
the sound of hard breathing
that surrounded it.
But even so,
I walked toward it
I felt as though I was being watched
by a thousand eyes.
It tasted
like a not yet ripe mango,
just the faintest taste
of what it should be.

Ryan Richardson

Floodgates

Your kiss is like a cool drink of water quenching
at first, but only for so long, after one sip I
yearn for more, burning passions flare up to a
blaze begging for some sort of release, a way to
quell this rising desire
It's intoxicating, a single one can never do,
nor can I settle for so little, because more is
what I want, what I need, it's a seduction I feel
the urge to feed, to give myself over to the pull
of the sparks held behind your lips, the parting
of them is like the ascent of a floodgate,
releasing it all in one big burst, the fire
washes over me consuming my body, enveloping my
whole being, every inch, every nerve is alive,
charged with feeling aware of every touch, the
power of your kiss washes over me, sweeping me
into your swirling pool of passion, gathering me
into your arms, covering me with a rush of cool water
temporarily subduing my thirst for you.

Nicole Yanolatos

Buying Doorknobs, Then Foundations
For Derek

Spending a spring dawn
in a fledgling orbit of confusion.
Stumbling, over the sands of this life
with the strains of new light,
my hands spread
over the length of the small of your
back while you sleep.

Without the backup singers,
when I'm alone, opened
and flat on Fate's stage,
I am subdued
by the fear of your reception.

Over your shoulder
the morning star is fading
and I am comforted by the finite.
Still, under the veneer and undisguised,
my tempo is allegretto
and I demand no boundaries.

Kelly Wheat

Naked Poem

We were sitting there
On the pavement
The loose cement making red dents
In my fingertips
And I said these words to him
"I love you"
"Yeah," he said
And suddenly I felt like that re-occurring nightmare
Standing in a crowd
Naked
Me, trying somehow to hide
My naked existence

But I couldn't
I couldn't hide
For he had already seen me
Naked inside my body

Cassandra Smith-Christmas

By the Sea

crouching there, I sink my finger into the wet sand,
soft and hard in the same moment;
carve the letters quickly, but carefully,
till words arise: I love her
step back then;
eager bullies, aggressive avengers, roll in and my words
disappear in a violent whitewash;
heart forgets to beat once, and once again
waves pull back confident;
but the words, like the beach, remain.
monstrous and empty Fate, manifested by the sea
angrier, she throws her hands upon them once more.
sliding back, revealing words, but only blurred, by hate.
crouch, and write them yet deeper, beckon Fate
to bury them or drown them in her cold depths.
deep into the night, and far into the morrow
for all of time we'll play this little game;
words written ever deeper and Fate ever angrier,
we'll play this little game by the sea.

Jason McCall

Upon Whose Blood

I must transform by fire, this heat that was my soul's
Containment
Return me to my ash so I might not be lost; interred
First, brush my dusty countenance upon the surface of a simple
Jar
Then, tend me to the fire to bond upon the vessel's form
Now, hard; cast down this urn and gather up the fragments
These shards reshape in energy the fashion of my memory
They can no more be reassembled as myself
Than life itself can be contained
So, worry not that I've escaped the tyranny of womb to worm
And scatter wide this broken vessel's flesh for time to work its
Will
In that—in turn—my quest will fall complete
Embrace this soil and you will know how kindred is the land
Upon whose blood all origins converge
Make blossoms of our veins and bones

Martin Kim

Disappearance
(Written in Amsterdam, Holland)

So I decided to disappear for a while . . .
Life in the city can make you crazy.
I needed a change of scenery.
A world encased in glass. Some place far.
No one knows my name here.
I am among the many merely passing through.
And still I belong!
To what I am uncertain, but the feeling of
Acceptance dwells within.
The longing for change is evident in my eyes.
The rain that falls steady here speaks of a change to come.
But what changes need I so terribly?
I want desperately to discover . . . so I decided
To disappear for a while.

Barbara Ann Pascarello

The Breath of Innocence

I used to lie on the grass and watch the clouds move,
And I held my teddy bear so tight when I heard lightning.
I could pick a rose and smell its beauty,
And looking a stranger in the eye wasn't so frightening.

I could question my life with reassurance and common sense,
And I could cry and scream for attention.
I could laugh a true laugh for all it was worth,
And the smell of my pillow equaled perfection.

I thought boys were the absolute root of all evil,
And danger would always be lurking in their hearts.
I didn't know how to put my dress on without ripping my tights
And mastered jealously like it was an art.

But now those memories grow rusty
And are replaced with the musky smell of incense.
I breathe in the fumes and close my eyes
And say goodbye to my innocence.

Melissa Jones

Impression Sunrise

I should be depressed, seated
here in this candle-lit room, a book
of Keyon sprawled on my lap. Me behind
these panes which rain and sleet
unavailingly pelt. Instead, I think of
the man Monet, and how he would have painted

you; a wisp of brown for your
hair, a daub of peach for your
soft skin. Seated in a canoe, skipping
across the suggestion of waves, you
paddle toward the crest of
the orange ball of sun to
catch it as it comes up.

Ryan Vine

almost home

now i see where your stains've left me
i touch those cracks between us and,
calluses intact, i put first one digit then
another into mouth till i
stuff the whole hand in there raw
(my cigarette's gone out again. i still see your streets.)
in the rushing up of meeting face to
clear i can sense you in the
periphery, i can see me straight ahead
(got to keep turning up the dial though i come back to it and
the sound of myself's too loud for my ears.)
and maybe i'm just sucking on a filter here but
i think i can see lights never existed i can
see my fingers spread now, just about distinct
i hold nothing but this that's in my hand
chanting: it's almost clear now
it's almost clear now
i'm pushing words together
form some sentences but see
i never was almost home

m. lisi

The Edge of Marriage

Down in the soul
Where angels sleep
And glass tears break,
My body aches with life.

I live in God's basement,
And the walls know my secrets.
Your cold eyes
Keep winter in my heart.

I split myself in two,
One for me,
One for you,
Silence dripping with hate.

I walk with no life,
No hope, no dreams.
I melt into the dark
To unlock my cage.

A life without love
Is a pity.
Love without life
Is hell.

Patrick Shine

Untitled

Heavens no,
I say again at 4 AM,
typing because typing
simulates action.

Impotent to knowledge
of the child I may be losing
to extenuating circumstance.

Useless to pathologize,
inscribe imperatives.

"Detach yourself,
barren woman,
from the child you did not bear
who called you mother."

I fear this loss
would be immune to poetry.

I fear the return
to a childless life
would hold not freedom
but poverty.

Katherine G. Audi

Cinderella Dreams

Tears rolling off my cheeks
Steady drip falling to the floor
The rhythmic beat putting me to sleep
Putting my thoughts into serenity

Looking out the crystal window
Rainbows galore brighten my face
Butterflies dancing on the sill
But gray clouds cover utopia

Jerking to awareness from crying gasps
Reality strikes once again
No longer a drip but now a steady stream
Flowing off the tip of my nose

Wishing my life was
Like my Cinderella dreams
But realizing dreams can come true
If I create the

Carla Dropiewski

Hot Days

The heat is intense
Suffocating and overwhelming
Nothing slakes my thirst
Neither tea nor coffee
Soothe the burning in my throat
Beer is useless
And soft drink even more so
The tap water is tepid
And smells of excess chlorination
The slow sweeping of the fan
Dries up my sweat
But does not cool me
And when the weather finally changes
It will take days
For the heat
To seep out of the walls

John Duckmanton

City Child

I had stopped, this night, at a corner where the traffic lights
flaunt their tricolour blooms in monotonous cycles.
I noticed the child as she stood, her bare feet clasping the
pavement, her short dressing gown revealing pale limbs
like the stems of sun-starved seedlings.
Her face was sharp, honed perhaps by a knowledge of the
alleyways.
In a world of bitumen and towering glass,
she watched the hurrying crowd, unconscious of their buffeting,
and scanning faces anxiously; whom did she seek?
Sometimes she glanced upwards where the god Neon
embroidered the midnight sky with garish dogmas.

How I wish that child the tenderness of grass beneath her feet,
soft foliage to brush her hands.
But most I wished her a blossom tree
to cast confetti petals on her sad scarecrow hair.

The lights changed. The cars behind me registered impatience.
Guilty in my warm comfort I pressed the accelerator,
knowing I would be haunted by the small figure
remaining in the petrol fumes of her concrete chasm where the
warehouses reared like sandstone cliffs in a dark forest of
factories.

Phyllis Telfer

The Azure Kingfisher

Magnificent, majestic, graceful
It's easy to admire this master at work
He hovers, then strikes
A flash of orange and electric blue
Such a fine use of nature's palette
He sits, head bobbing
All day long eyeing the water
And occasionally eyeing you

Troy Phelps

Far to the Right of Magic

Between the pauses of reality's blend,
A hand reached out tapping me on the shoulder,
With a voice that was surprising in clarity,
More than just a prayer of bells ringing to please,
But the lilt of a blarney stone well-kissed.

A laughing angel with swan white wings,
Fluttering around inside my mind,
Or is the air blessed with the Devil's charm,
With a chuckling shivering kiss,
Keeping me there longer than I ever planned.

Always to remain a mystery this whisper,
Of a land far away in the heart of promises,
Never to be given in the seduction of tomorrow,
In the landscape deeper than a sigh,
Of greener fields far to the right of magic.

This is but a moment in a busy day,
An idle wanderer caught in the light,
Closing eyes to savour a friendly chime,
A pearl polished by the grains of days,
More than just a little grey.

Martin Enticknap

One Day in May

"The war's over," the woman said and shook her coal black hair
And minced across the cobbled street past the slavering butcher
And the boy's humour coursed with expectancy of cream buns
And money for the pictures

"The war's over," the uncle said and put sugar on his porridge
And read the Derby odds and waited for tea to pour
And the boy sat still in admiration of the cat unwashed by water
And serenely unschooled

"The war's over," the teacher said and pointed at the blackboard
Weapon held high as a soldier of destiny
Milquetoast to the leery stares of the unclean encamped before
Him who still had to drink milk

"The war's over," the politician said and remember not an inch
And the airman polished his cap badge and dreamt of
Million-dollar legs
And the boy saw the woman with coal black hair kissing the
Butcher and felt the threat of bedtime

Brian Campbell

Coffee Shop Faint

"You're a special kind of girl,"
he said without conviction.
His voice came to me distant, stilted, strangled.
I looked at his disconnected smile.
I didn't want to hear him lie to me,
but he wouldn't stop.
"I think I'm in love with you," he continued
and his eyes glazed over like a doughnut.
I wanted to scream.
I tried to punch him as hard as I could,
right on his fatuous, beakish nose
but it ended up a flirtatious feint.
He caught my fist, pried it flat, held my now-limp hand,
"Are you listening to me? I said I think I love you."
He repeated pointlessly, twice, "I love you."
(His voice was as hollow as the words it carried.)
I started to fade, then: the airless coffee shop disintegrated,
what could I do but float away?
It was his fault, anyway, he started it:
you should mean it if you say a thing like that.

Rebekah Rachel McCoy

Old Lady Sheds Tears on TV

The lady on TV with the tattooed makeup
Cries for Jesus, some long-winded exaltation
About charity and the dues of life.
I think the crying is her profession;
The makeup, unsmearing, tells me so.
She sits with sticky, hardened hair that reaches toward Heaven
Or the airborne mic, it's hard to tell which anymore.
The crusted mane hides the hose
That fills her mold with water not so holy.
Before the show, sitting in a high chair,
Getting sprayed and combed and glitzed.
Rehearsing in her head a monologue titled "Sinful Vanity."
A celebrity of Jesus.
She's sitting on stage, crying, rambling on about our duty to
Pay, our duty to love the Man who sits atop her hair.
I can't help but feel detached from this plastic doll.
When I was little, I wanted one of those dolls that wetted or
Cried when you squeezed its belly. Now I have one.
I can't help but repel the demands to love Jesus from
This painted woman who cries because the cue cards tell her to.

Jada L. Ach

View from an Unwashed Kitchen Window

The fence grew tired of its mass
And fell that way.
The trellis, with its impartial view,
Perceived the need for balance
And fell this way.
Nodding camellias rustled their dry leaves,
Applauding the composition.
Beneath the stone Buddha,
The daffodil lay quietly,
Breathing in a shallow way.
The gardener,
Who once cared,
Lives somewhere else now.

Thomas Law

School

How can you write poetry about school?
(such a dead
topic)
which
closes out the rain and
measures it when it stops.
Six-and-one-half hours
blocking the sunlight
in the name of
the Roman Empire and
the square root of
sixty-two
sea gulls.
Assaulted by
boys who know
they'd be better off at the sea.

Emily Cobb

My Father's Voice

Upon pulling into the cracked driveway
I started thinking of the time when you
Cautioned me to wait, and that making due
Would benefit no one. Ending each day
With regretful sighs was an ending for
True desire. And as my pockets jingle
I think of him, and the money that lingered
In some hidden safe or secret drawer.
Adding up my bills in desperation,
I think of him, and how he went without
In secret, while kindly bearing the brunt
Of my false appreciation. And now,
I laugh at myself, as my own son
Tosses expressionless pennies around.

Jeffrey Myers

Fan Dance

In the Iowa State Fair tent
where I'm not supposed
to go, my fingers lift
nickels to slots.
Whistles trill
and photos flicker their
tales. When lights burst
from the view piece
of the last row play box,
I gaze as Sally sways
with her ostrich feathers. Here
is knowledge not for one
in a red 6X dress who must stand
on a box to see. Then Sally bares
nothing but legs. Sex stays veiled.
I slip in one more coin.

D. Jane Hall

Artist's Profile
Rohee Dasgupta
Kolkata, India

"Faces!" is an introspection of the self; it's a critical perspective of the myriad roles one plays subtly on life's stage, yet remains true to the subjective mind that ultimately finds it out. I have a B.A. in English Literature, Calcutta University, and recently got an offer of study from the University of Hull, UK, for M.A. in International Politics. I have a keen interest for philosophy, the fine arts, sociology, cultural anthropology, psychology, history, language, and literature (English and French). I've been a freelancer in the popular daily "The Statesman" since 1996 and have completed research work on "Masks of the Word," an anthropological study to be published shortly.

Faces!

Whenever my eyes face yours,
Your face leaps into color,
Odd color that comes and goes . . .
Almost like a chameleon flicker
Of winter sun or mists of poignant love
Of that brick bridge, over there!
Rising above the railings, which seem to scratch and bar
Rare glimpses of the sky,
Your face turns rays, like an opal . . . wading,
Like soft sepia bubbles bursting sometimes
In my daylight dreams, in some third dimension
Where not living I really live.
Yet when I rip off the dyed masks, the clinging veneer
In a sudden standstill calm, seeing
Through all your faces,
I see one face, your face . . .
Your true face!

Rohee Dasgupta

Artist's Profile
Placide Saul Severe
Cupertino, CA, USA

The poem "Bleach Junkies" is about the human condition in regards to the unattainable, yet ever alluring state of perfection. As humans, we desire what is pure, yet are willing to settle for what is not, and then choose to convince ourselves that it is in order to escape the fact that purity is beyond our efforts alone. My band NRAEVIS performs music that expounds upon such concepts and ideas. NRAEVIS means "an act of willful intent by means of music."

Bleach Junkies

Apathetic, we bathe with soiled intent for
purity. I ask how, while she sings why, and
they write books on when the unknown
perfection is made just that.
Ruined by the knowledge that beauty can be
that much brighter and the sole purpose more
noble, I sit chasing the desire for a
righteousness whispered by my
acknowledgement of the human condition
served in regret. Paved black with white
spots, furry and round clothed in stark
brutality, the people churn. Together, we lust
for that elusive, perhaps that pervasive,
yet sexy perfection. And when it comes, we
won't know, but we hope that we'll keep
caring so as not to be left to face who we
have been, who we are, and who we want to
be.

Placide Saul Severe

Artist's Profile
Kathleen Tara Macken
San Marcos, CA, USA

Teachers are our biggest asset and their ability open our minds often goes unnoticed, so I must give credit where credit is due, to three teachers, who without this poem wouldn't have been written or rewritten and made better. Thank you, Mr. Trupe, for the homework assignment, and especially Ms. Houssen and Mr. Pellergrino for supporting and encouraging my creativity and seeing something in me that I didn't know existed. Thank you, thank you!

WWI

The benevolence is masked by dead blood.
The droning of the dead and decaying is far too familiar.
I have ransacked my insides,
But have found nothing but a rank and rotted spirit.
I am numb to the wails of the hurt and dying.
The gunpowder that I used to smell
Is now embroidered into my soul like a religion.
My heart still pounds through my chest,
Yet it pounds like the enigma of an abyss.
The phantoms that haunt the trenches
Lie in pools of merciless blood and bullets on the field.
With impact of body and bullet,
I feel the implosion beginning to take place.
The residual effect of the bullet with my name on it
Will be the nameless, faceless stench of another corpse.

Kathleen Tara Macken

Artist's Profile
Marion May Campbell
Melbourne, Australia

The poem explores the way death stalks the speech of a depressed person. It's as if each utterance slowly, painfully launched on its way staggers off, curls up, and is silenced in white, trackless oblivion. The symptom in turn becomes the patient; her sentences are like so many blanked out inmates whose gazes fail to intersect and which become freak exhibits for the sane. I hope that anyone who has ever been deeply depressed or witnessed depression might, paradoxically perhaps, connect with the emotion behind the poem.

Depressed Woman Talking

Like Plath's sheep in fog
Her sentences step off
Into blankness
Lose their footprints
So that each
Is isolated
In lambency
End-stopped
Snow-gagged

One after the other
Her reflections
Appear
To stares below
Like mental patients
In each of many
Mullioned windows

Such beautiful autisms
Their clear features
Utterly
Bereft

Marion May Campbell

Artist's Profile
David William McPherson
Toronto, ON, Canada

I wrote this poem following a weekend retreat my wife and I took for our one-year wedding anniversary in May 2001. The beauty of the natural surroundings during an afternoon hike and my beautiful wife trekking beside me were my muse. I live in Toronto, Ontario, Canada. I have enjoyed writing poetry as a hobby for the last ten years.

Meandering Thoughts by the Maitland River

Love lingers in the woods above the banks.
Below, fly fishermen cast their love
waist-deep in the placid waters, hoping for a bite.

The late afternoon sun glistens and reflects the dreams of all
who call this wooded wonder their home.

Above, hikers climb a trail to new altitudes and new attitudes,
longing to stay one more moment in this peaceful retreat,
away from the clanging and banging,
hurrying and scurrying of the city streets.

Birds beckon them and welcome the visitors to their sanctuary.
Back down on the banks,
the Canada geese rest in the grassy reeds in the reflective pool;
no flight tonight for these symbols of Canadiana.

The lovers pause and ponder about the year gone by:
friends forsaken, family taken.
Memories like a fire burning flicker and flame.
Smiles leave their shadows on the forest floor.

Fishing for love and fishing for life,
Lovers and strangers find hope in the waters,
And the woods warm the soul on a May Maitland day.

David William McPherson

Artist's Profile
Julia Abreu
New York, NY, USA

Born in Porto, Portugal, I have resided in Manhattan, New York City most of my life, where for thirty-one years I worked for a major international airline. Having left that life in 2000, I continued to pursue more avidly my passion for poetry which always derives from the intensity I feel for all aspects of life. My favorite hobbies are foreign languages.

The Exhibit

"Flowered breast with suspicious
undertone shadows," they said, Thursday
on the phone, asking her to return.
All she thought about was dying,
that weekend when she slept so cold
and no one heard, no one saw the old
pantomime, the sentence setting her apart.
She hung like an exhibit
in a gallery on 64th Street cutting
second avenue two floors under,
an unclear radiology picture,
a murky negative painting.
The heart wilted below her feet
and the breath froze with delivering
steps of enamel rumors she recognized,
a recurring nightmare, that persona
with the particular queer smell
that picked at her life for days,
she bruised against it, waiting
in the hollow of day sweats until Monday.

Julia Abreu

We Have Never Been Damsels in Distress

For my muse, Vincent Millay

We have never been damsels in distress.
Enchantment shan't impose ill-gotten sleep.
Although thorned stems drag on our breast,
I shall be bleeding, not a dust-covered heap.
Never bite fruit unless pluck'd from our boughs.
Tadpoles in jars aren't for kisses or vows.
Bob my wild splitting hair 'fore his ascent.
Our slender fingers stay bare by consent.
And if blossom's juice be smear'd on our lid,
We'll capture Puck - play our mischief instead.
Charm'd defiance; shan't my touch be forbid-
We dance past midnight, then fall into bed.
Sun bruises sky as it falls to the ground,
Tender lips, scorched by day, poised as a frown.
On this swollen night, must breath remain bound?
Suffer me, Vincent, to unhook your gown.

Lenora Duvall

Untitled

Back when fresh-cut grass smell
meant skin freckling in white tank tops
and skinny dipping with neighborhood boys
on nights when the air felt thick
and made our foreheads damp, eyelashes dewy;
when voices drifted in from other houses
and barbecuing was something we did
for the night;
and cars lined back streets and
cousins slept in sleeping bags on our floors,
with my eyes closed and your letter in my hand,
I turned around and found our last forever.

Hilary Ann Smith

Sidewalk Paradigm

The girl at the health food store
is as thin as grass.
Smooth darkness shades her face.
Her hair is brown with red streaks.
She returns his change
from lucid hands on frail bones
that hold the key to who he was.
He knows that.
She reads his awe and smiles.
His hair is thin as a baby's and grey.
He sees women more clearly
now that he's become invisible
like all their fathers,
grey in the corner humming.
He remembers everything when it costs less,
post-Depression nostalgia.
He loves Roosevelt like he knew him
and remembers the value of Eleanor.
One A-bomb wasn't enough for Truman.
From ignorance he delivered two.

Michael J. Bono

A Loss

This scab
have had on leg skin
eyesore that erupts pulse
through deep tissue, where
still a decent pain reminds
of a dirty fall.
Stretchy mandibular contortions,
atypical wailing and pointed at it penitent eye in response
a quaint sight
this scab, where little cells
work frantically, an
epithelial revelry
where a cell reproduces with itself until
old flesh is new flesh,
cell families joined in community healing,
in mourning and in mending,
until a memory of clumsy instant and some botched skin
is all that's left. Small
superficial stain; tactile requiem,
scar tissue to recall beating instant

Nicolo Roberto Marra-Biggs

Galganooza

Infrared sky locaters
sold cheaply on portobello
sultry, sultry the soot night hovers,
the beast of Galganooza
sleeps and groans in the city's underbelly.
Albion, lost city of imagination.
The sky is lost to light.
And she walks by again,
all dimpled and bulbous
ankles desperate to escape
stilettos arching outwards.
flesh spills and fights with fabric.

The alley is dark. "Shh," she hisses,
"tonight you're a rich man and I'm a star."

Rebecca Jane Keys

Alone in Her Memory

Early in the morning, the market place bustles.
Coins rattling in buyers' pockets,
children rushing towards the bakery.
He walks alone and remembers.
She would visit every stand with a joyful "Hello!"
She would feed the lone dog in the alley
with the leftovers of her cinnamon raisin danish.
He recalls how the years rolled by, and their family grew.
Ringing of gleeful laughter, children prancing around
in her tulip-filled garden.
Her voice, soft as an angel,
serenading the children to sleep.
Her dress slowly swaying back and forth in perfect unison
with the pendulum of her grandfather clock.
The children grew and said their goodbyes.
He reminisces the way they grew old together, the recipes
she so adored seemed empty
without a full table to critique them.
The way she grew weary,
the color of her Clinique rouge cheeks
the twinkle in her deep blue eyes, never fading.
Her home became a house to accommodate one man.
Her memory never left his side.

Zil Dilip Patel

First Snow Fall

The bitterness of the pale breeze
The slippery wet pond began to freeze
Milky white satin covers the ground
Icicles illuminate sparkling in sound

Dreamy palette of color grey
Let all of the children begin to play
Dancing and making angels sigh
Family gathers to hear rain cry

Having the first snowfall
Has made everyone begin to call
Joyous in laughter of memories
Looking at the Christmas trees

Reflections of lights and smiles
Firewood and pine cone piles
We all love to see such a sight
Especially the first snowfall night

Pamela Jean Hildebrand

Walking the Walls

I stroll the halls and spacious
rooms of a fine museum,
my eyes as big as Moon Pies.
I scoot on my knuckles and knees,
primate-descended proud.
I crawl on my stomach
ingesting talent like a silkworm
weaving a shroud.
I imagine myself the painter
squeezing light from a tube,
observing the thickness of tint
carefully applied.
But I am merely the paid critic,
a lover of the requirement,
walking the walls,
telling just enough truth
to sting but stay ruination.
Art is its own abyss,
deep enough, wide enough,
to invite plunging.

Noah du Halcyon

Desert Sun

The day's heat was thrust upon us like a
leaping tiger upon an unsuspecting zebra.
But unlike our striped sympathizers, we have
already come to grips and accepted our
fates. The days drain on hour after hour,
our happiness drained ounce by ounce. The
flies buzz all around, conducting a constant
swarming assault on our patience. Madness
seems like a possible destination to this
trip, but even the fall into insanity must be
considered an unapproved escape from this
hell, for it also stays just out of reach.
But there is a light on the horizon. It
grows brighter every day, and its warmth
increases the already unbearable numbers on
the thermometer. Its source is unknown, but
without an answer, hope is still possible.
So we drag on through the sand and sun
dreaming of better days ahead. Ones where
time goes too fast, for a change.

Joshua R. Christensen

Without Wings

Today I felt like flying
But I found I had no wings
And my sorrows came again
So my hopeless soul hit rock bottom.
The sun seemed dull
My beckoning dreams so far away
The love in your embrace nonexisting
Every joy turned to hopelessness.
Tears of remorse flow daily
My heart is growing cold from hurt
I need a meaning for existence
But I have come to realize that there is none.
You are the only light in my being
The only smile on my face
The only beat of my heart
And as these beads of sorrow fall down my cheeks
I admit that I can't go on
I am just too tired . . .

Suzie Kathryn Harris

More Than Skin

Terrified and tumbling
I felt like more than your body
Wrapped and tight,
bound by pale skin and black hair
hands touching

I am more than a body
more than your muse
I sweep silently by
not missing anything
feeling like light

Patient, persuading
elevated beyond the sky
your mind weighs heavy
makes earthquake steps
I am more than your body

Poets say the soul
resides outside the frame
My memory is strong,
remembers before breath
We aren't the same

Karen Coffman

the bony ribs of jason

i left the bony ribs of jason
for the fruit
of my own
personal desire
its scent still heavy
upon my flesh
my absence still
thorn
to his side
but now how my belly
hollows and aches
craving seed
craving kisses
but outside the road hisses
and i find myself
packing girlishness
in an old leather bag
love stepping lightly
away from the door

Nat Chrastman

Vidyapati's Final Song

She cries when Krishna leaves. The forest wakes
  to haloed dew around the still-warm camp.
Radha's heart congeals like cooling wax
as Krishna's promise to return is dampened
  by the morning air. Her husband never
  sees her suffer. Radha milks and feeds
  the cows, praying Krishna won't forget
her soul and body graced beneath the trees.

I hear my Radha cry and send a thousand
  kisses. Every day I fail to write
a song that captures passion like her mouth,
full and blushing, echoing Krishna's smile,
divine as it is. I know my Radha breathes
for Krishna, not for life or men like me.

Gina Kim In

Untitled

It's a place where the seagulls dip low and fly high.
Endless space reaching out to the sunset sky.
Sand slips through my fingers as I bury my feet.
Then I dive to the depths to escape the great heat.
We wake up at dawn and run down to the beach.
This feast for the eyes leaves me without speech.
Family and friends stand side by side.
As sure as the comings and goings of tide.
Talent shows, mini-golf, memories are made.
Until stars come out and to bed we are laid.
The day before parting I'll look up at the moon.
Saying, this won't be the last time.
I'll be back someday soon.

Rebecca Harding Scott

Trust

My daughter drops
a small, lightweight toy
onto the soft, downy pillow
that is our cat's belly.
It disappears into the fur
and she giggles.
The cat raises
her ancient, deliberate gaze.
Her steady, measured eyes,
almost buried
in the fluff of her face,
belie how fragile
she is in the shadow
of a seven-year-old's
looming innocence.
What I see is
a history of maternal impulses,
and how the boundary of trust
has been again, extended . . .
out into love.

Mary Rose Sullivan

The Jungle Lies Wherever We Go

We journey to a place where peacocks lay eggs
encrusted with silver and green and kiss

the cheeks of soldiers, like us,
turning their hair into mane.

Let us be lazy and soulful,
taking long naps under the canopy branches.
The bark of these trees is drenched
in mossy scum,
but I kissed it anyway,
and these rosebuds sprouted from my tongue.
So fertilize my lips, please.

We are warriors seeking to conquer love.
Bottle the spiced perfume of the jungle
so it can be spread across the flesh of human necks.
Be brave. Step inside to breathe in inalienable love.

Rinse my eyelids clean with the muck from this swamp
and fill your navel with wild orchids.
Come. Let me discover what it's like between
the tropics and your skin.
We shall hide in the tall, tall grass.

Alisha Desai

Moving On

He had lined her black,
garbage-bagged stuff
up to the doorway as if
she'd take worn items

to her other home. He says,
"Kids took most. This, trash."
Outside his family room door,
Birds of Paradise bloom

like peacock feathers spread
as his backrest. She loved gardens,
mitten-toed cats, and him.
Her paintings hang as mirrors

of multi-scenic lives: kids, cats,
portraits, and photoscapes, stuff.
Their new sofa, white and
welcoming, not worn, will be.

Henry Greenfield

Born Beneath a Full, Blue Moon

Her young mind conceiving innocent expressions
Felt through colors on paper
All of her creative inventions
Eager to learn from constant observation
Finding truth and reason
When discoveries lead to recreation
Deliverance of infinite curiosity
Unveils beauty in her endless understanding
Undimmed energies glow
Forming her newborn spirituality
An intoxicating surge of emotions
Display her unfiltered innocence
Forever healed by this comforting unity
She is my strength and devotion
Though, upon chance of reborn doubt
Her gentle kiss upon my cheek
Is heartfelt bliss I'd surely die without

Amethyst Rose Hargreaves

Unsatisfied

New York City in the full moonlight
this lunacy touches more than just the crazy people
my mind racing through its memories
I wonder if she even knows I'm still alive
walking the streets of poets and button men
the city is a muse for the wicked and the gifted
trying to stay clear of the backwater swill
that carries men down to the unfathomed deeps
and all the wind-up dolls on wheels
the cogs in the wheel
spinning gold into the pockets of the shiny ones
for all the pretty little things
how we love the pretty little things
promising elusive happiness
remaining ever unsatisfied

Chris Barczynski

Counting Sheep

He filled his cart with wares before each sun
began to rise, and wearily he pondered
pending drudgery in disguise. He wiped the
sweat above his brow and held his chin up
high. His fingers bled, above his head was
heard a bleary sigh. He pushed his cart all
over town and knocked on endless doors,
in hopes the next was welcoming, more
than the one before. He barely earned, and
often burned to crucify his plight. Although
he yearned, he soon returned; another
sleepless night. Until he failed to rise one
day and gather wares of old. His spirit weak,
his heart grew meek, his hands were chafed
and cold. The task that lay before me was
so rightly understood. Though true but sad,
I too have had a bitter childhood. I carefully
packed the loyal wares, prepared for my
depart. The day I held my chin up high and
pushed my father's cart.

Kimberly Joy Dollhouse

The Wishing Lake

Sometimes I sing at night
and the reeds sway
like lonely widows. Frosted
images of lovers hide
behind the liquid windows
of tiny houses; pitched
pebbles sink into the blue
dungeon. Dew dampens my back
when I lay on the grass,
arms around an invisible form.

I dip my toes in the water
and puff on a menthol cigarette.
With my sword of light,
I fight like a wounded soldier,
egrets and herons cheer
from the mangroves. I dance
along the shore, under a cashew
moon, leaves float
like green angels and empty
beer bottles rise to the surface.

Wayne Anthony Loshusan

Antidote

So soothing at first, a warm summer rain.
Enveloped like this, I feel so safe.
The rain freezes, I find myself shivering.
Ice never felt this cold.
The storm returns to paradise, its heaven.
But it's gone again before I blink.
The anxiety makes me dizzy.
Do you feel my pulse racing?
Your poison is pumping through my veins.
Reality is slipping away.
Will you save me from your deadly kiss,
Or will you leave me here to drown
In this pool of blissful ignorance?
I'm getting close to the end now.
Everything is fuzzy and surreal.
I've slipped beneath the surface.
The light above is becoming harder to reach.
The darkness below is tightening its hold.
My fate is in your hands, please rescue me.
Your antidote is toxic, but tastes so sweet.

Kerry Frances Ransom

Chocolaty Remembrance

With chocolate breath
we kissed
each other's sugared lips,
softer than butter.

In the silent sanctuary of our eyes,
silent
as a muffled winter morn,
there absorbed would be the sum of our surprise.

Gently nested here in my bosom
this memory will be warm,
crystallized in chocolate crumbs
long after the love is forlorn.

Leila Frances Wright

Unencumbered

When I am not burdened
by bag, or baby,
my hips sail from side to side,
encountering space
that would otherwise be left untouched.
These hips, these contours,
are meant to sway freely,
like the days before
herringbone pinched tender flesh
into exaggerated conformity,
and then,
expectations replaced physical constraints,
putting our whole selves
at risk of rejection.
Tear off your cerebral corset,
allow the intuitive curves
to dip and sway,
entering, enriching,
the space that would otherwise remain
none the wiser.

Miranda Marie Valentine

Scattered Pieces

Breathe in my scattered pieces
Slowly exhaling me
Feel this flow quite intrinsic
Each one representing my dynasty

A force quite tangible
Impulses come together
Making me beautiful
Learning my language

Entwined energies
Connecting to the wholeness
Letting go; don't hold back
Breathe in my scattered pieces

Melanie E. Rodgers

The Memories of Life

By the light of the candles' glow
Romeo and Juliet are writing
In the town below
Julius Caesar is inviting

Then he had a memory
Of a dream
He saw a beautiful teacher
Flowing downstream

She turned into a creature
That lived in the ocean
That lives in the coral reef

Then she had a sense of emotion
A sense of moral grief
This mermaid was pallid
She started to sing this sad ballad

Samantha Michelle Bernaerts

Loneliness

Ashes across the misty mountain stream
Yearning for a presence no longer earthly
A seed planted much too deep to reach the sun's inviting rays
Young souls search for wisdom
A being too withered with grief to grasp reality
Wind whispers songs of hope that can no longer be heard
The rain from the heavens hide tears of time wasted
Gray tree lines cry out for attention
From those who wish to seek it
Yet the bewildered can no longer hear its cry
To have loved so deeply is triumphant
To have fallen so low is sorrowful
An empty shell once full of creativity
Longs to be among the ashes in the misty mountain breeze

Marilee Joanne Foster

Summer of '76

During the sizzling sun of a hot summer day,
We carelessly ripped, roared down the windy dirt road.
In my apple-hued Ford ragtop,
Gripping the steering wheel tightly, as the wind flowed.
Previously, we had frolicked away from our farm duties,
Only to act like heathens as we soared up
And down the sandy route.
It had been a very drawn out, weary July's day,
Hence the long-filled winter drought.
As I conducted my car through a narrow-sided turn,
I noticed something yonder as it glistened.
It was cube shaped, possibly a cardboard box,
My passenger saw it too, from her words I listened.
"Faster! Faster!" she encouraged me,
With the clutch to the floor, I shifted to fifth gear.
We approached it at a rapid speed,
With only two feet away, the box started to clearly appear.
Two inches away, our adrenaline rushed as we flew so immensely,
At the last second, I swerved not to collide.
Fate struck that day as I reached for my rearview mirror,
Looking back at the box . . . a boy climbed out the side.

Tricia Ann Linenberger

Capture

Winds have carried me many miles,
to a new lens in galaxy's time.
Sweeping soul-sore memories aside.

Trusting but one photographer,
glossy tears now overdeveloped.
Horizons of past hues no longer blind me.

Gently fading like a stored-away photo,
surrounded by boxed boundaries.
Self-made walls where I no longer reside.

I give to you my weathered camera,
cherish the true spirit inside.
Grasp my view and capture the real me.

Kristal Lynne Gerberick

Lead On, My Love, and I Shall Follow Thee

Until at restful river's bank reclined
As Orpheus after Eurydice.
Before this correspondence 'cross the sea
Each typing finger longed to tell the mind:
Lead on, my love, and I shall follow thee.
When bit by bit our hearts could feel as free
As soaring larks because your words, refined
As Orpheus' after Eurydice,
Transformed the waking world's hue for me.
Each rose-tinged sunrise beckoned, undeclined;
Lead on, my love, and I shall follow thee!
But after dancing, singing merrily,
In distant lands our dream remains confined
As Orpheus' after Eurydice.
Yet words for us grow sweet with melody,
To dearer songs than nearer hearts can find;
Lead on, my love, and I shall follow thee
As Orpheus after Eurydice.

Alex S. Little

Regret

Looking upon the gathering of baby blue
Shards huddled in a black dustpan, the reflections of
Time passing with hands of a naked clock cause
Tears to absorb back into turquoise eyes having once

Fallen toward a molten core only
Saved from oblivion by filthy linoleum
While the mind gasps for oxygen deprived

Via tracheal blockage from the reentering of
Foolish words accidentally breaking the speed of sound

Alerting you to the desperate need of the
Heimlich of forgiveness.

Brad Wadl

Sudden Memories

Your scent lingers in the air,
I smile as it enters my body, my soul.
You flow through every vein, every bone,
I close my eyes and take in as much as I can.

Your firm hand gently touches my face,
Flows down through my hair,
Touching every strand.
I stare in to the depths of your eyes,
Reading every emotion trapped within them.
The gentle caress of your lips,
Sends the deepest shivers of pure enchantment,
Dancing underneath my skin.
Enticing my love to abandon all morals.
Our souls are entangled with obsession,
As we express our intimate passions.

I exhale . . .
Releasing the sweet scent that I unwillingly longed for,
My damp eyes open, and the memory is erased.
As the smell slowly vanished,
The memory followed in its trace.

Nicolette Elieen Macagnone

The Stranger

The two walked slowly, brooding,
Heads bowed, shoulders bent,
As if searching for lost hope,
Code-written in the sand.
They spoke not a word.
Why speak? The only world they knew
Collapsed in bitter shame and grief
But days ago.
Ignoring a passing stranger,
They marched grimly on to nowhere;
Oblivious to everything but their fierce-felt pain.
How could they know the robe-clad peasant
They had scarcely seen
Had walked on stars, designed the Milky Way,
And manufactured every tiny grain of sand
On which they walked that day?

Wes G. Hunt